Cuba 54

*It's Time To End 54 Years of Abuse
of 11 Million People At The Hands of
The Miami Cartel*

PAUL LEBON

Cuba 54

*It's time to end 54 years of abuse of 11 million people
at the hands of the Miami Cartel*

By

PAUL LEBON

Dedicación

Por la presente, dedico este libro a todos mis maravillosos amigos en Cuba. Gracias a todos por su amor, apoyo, aliento y amistad. Aquí está la esperanza de una vida mejor Yo amo a todos.
Y quiero compartir mi corazón con Idriana, Reinaldo, Odlie y Sara.

I hereby dedicate this book to all my wonderful friends in Cuba. Thank you all for your love, support, encouragement and friendship. Here's hoping for a better life. I love everyone. And I share my heart with Idriana, Reinaldo, Odlie, and Sara.

Reposar en Paz
Rest in Peace
Daniela y Nitza

Table of Contents

Prologue

Friends in High Places

In the year 2000, I had arranged for a teacher and two students from David G. Burnett Elementary School in Dallas where I was a volunteer tutor to greet President Clinton as he stepped off Air Force One at Dallas Love Field. I took my nine-year-old son Jared along to see Air Force One from behind the fence. When the White House Advance Team saw him they offered to also let him onto the tarmac to greet the president.

In 2008 I went back to my former home of New Hampshire for the Presidential Primary, a quadrennial road trip. I went to speaking events featuring both GOP and Democratic candidates. I was well positioned at Nashua High School North to get a word in with then Senator Barack Obama.

In 2011 Luis my assistant in Cuba was looking through my laptop pictures and came upon these two and was beside himself with excitement. Everywhere we would go he would tell people, "Paulo know President Clinton and Obama."

So Cubans started asking me to speak to 'my friends' about their plight. I doubt that I can get face time with President Obama busy as he is, but I am devoting this book to the cause of the 11 Million people of Cuba. They deserve to have their side heard and to have the injustices perpetrated against them by the Miami Cartel exposed. Here's hoping that a copy of this book eventually makes its way to President Obama.

Introduction

I am a New England native, grandson of Belgian and Canadian immigrants. The primary language in my home, school, and church growing up was French. I can speak conversational Spanish, originating with high school classes and developed over the years through travel and living in Texas. So why am I writing a book about Cuba and its decades of abuse suffered as a result of the US embargo?

My interest in Cuba goes back almost a quarter-century. In the late 1980s as an airline marketing executive, I traveled there with a friend. We flew to Toronto and utilized interline agreements to secure transportation to Havana on Air Canada. That trip was simply a couple of single guys looking for a relaxed good time, and indeed we found one.

Since then I have maintained a mild interest, but over the past three years my approach to and view of Cuba has changed dramatically. My overall opinion of Cuba after multiple visits is that it is a World-Class country with a Third World mindset and infrastructure. It has tremendously resourceful and friendly people and wonderful natural attributes including spectacular beaches and mountains. If its potential could be developed the country could become a world-class leader in the Caribbean.

Several years ago on Facebook I accidentally befriended a Cuban national who had the same name as a friend of mine. Looking to do something productive with my free time after a nine-month tortuous divorce saga, I reached out to my Facebook friend to make contact with the Catholic Church in Cuba on my behalf. I wanted to travel to Cuba in a missionary capacity supporting the efforts of the Church and evangelizing to young people. President Obama had loosened travel restrictions so I traveled to Cuba on a religious travel license.

That effort led to multiple trips and activities, including volunteering at a Liturgy celebrated by Pope Benedict XVI. I met and befriended hundreds of individuals. Some of them such as my assistant Luis Triana Moran have come to mean a great deal to me personally and I cherish them like family members. I met and developed cordial relationships with individuals who work within the Cuban Government. It's been an equal exchange in terms of information sharing, cultural exchange, and future hopes.

When I was diagnosed with Early Onset Alzheimer's and the US healthcare system offered little promise, I was treated at Cuba's CIREN (International Center for Neurological Restoration) Clinic for five weeks. The resulting 'pushback' of my Alzheimer's symptoms was stunning.

Through it all, I have realized that the Cuban people are warm, wonderful and gregarious, and they love to share fellowship with music, singing, and dancing. The country's literacy rate is higher than what one might expect at 99.9 percent, higher even than the United States[1]. The infant mortality rate is 4.83 per 1M, vs. 6 per 1M in the US.[2] - [3]

Yet Cuban citizens have one eternal question: *"Why do Americans hate us, and why do they keep the Bloqueo in place?"*

It is a question whose answer lies in the fact that some elected officials in Florida have a visceral hatred for the Castros because they ruined the criminal Dictatorship these people's families were part of and because some of their cronies prosper financially from the Embargo. This is the United States – so what else is new; scam the taxpayer anyway you can and package it as national security. In a country where some in office cannot speak three sentences without mentioning God, Jesus, or the Bible, how can elected officials be so hostile to 11 Million Cubans for 54 years?

---

1   *United Nations Development Programme Report 2011*
2   *indexmundi.com/cuba/infant_mortality_rate.html*
3   *indexmundi.com/united_states/infant_mortality_rate.html*

When Fidel Castro's forces were victorious at Santa Clara and Dictator Fulgencio Batista fled with virtually all of the country's cash reserves on Jan. 1, 1959, Batista's cronies, thugs, and henchmen were not far behind. They fled to avoid prosecution and likely firing squads for their crimes against the Cuban people under Batista's direction. But unlike Batista they came to the United States and created a government in exile with Miami as their capital. More important, they developed and controlled the narrative about what was taking place in Cuba under Castro. In many cases they were assigning to Castro's troops the very offenses they themselves had committed. These Batista exiles were the first spin doctors.

So for 54 years the exile community in Miami has controlled all the information regarding what has been taking place in Cuba. They have used that control to inflict suffering on the Cuban people in retaliation for the Cubans not having risen up to overthrow Fidel Castro.

Based on research and first-person accounts that have been compiled into this book, hopefully the tide will be able to turn for the 11 Million Cuban people.

Section I.
Bienvenido á Cuba

1. History of
The Embargo/Bloqueo (Blockade)

From this point forward this situation will be referred to strictly as the Blockade out of respect for and in unity with the good people of Cuba who suffer consequences of this policy every day of their lives. (Embargo in US; Blockade/Bloqueo in Cuba).

The original Blockade (Arms Embargo) was put in place on March 14, 1958 in support of Fidel Castro's Revolutionaries who were fighting to overthrow the Batista Dictatorship. As the Cuban military's ammunition fell short in supply and spare parts to repair their Air Force planes could not be obtained, the Cuban military went into a state of dysfunction and were defeated by Castro's troops on Jan. 1, 1959.[1]

The goal of the Revolutionaries had been to rid the country of the Dictator Fulgencio Batista and his cronies, along with the US Mafia and their casinos and bordellos. The struggle with Batista began on July 26, 1953 when Castro and his troops attacked the Moncada Barracks in Santiago along with the barracks in Bayamo. The raids were unsuccessful.

As a result of that action, Castro and his brother Raul were arrested and given lengthy prison sentences. Bowing to public pressure however, Batista pardoned the Castros and others in

---

1   *wikipedia.org/wiki/Cuban_Revolution*

1955. The brothers fled to Mexico where they titled their group the 26th of July Movement.

The Castros and 80 troops returned to Cuba in December 1956 aboard a 60' yacht called the Granma. This began two years of battles and skirmishes across the country. These hostilities culminated with the Battle of Santa Clara on Dec. 31, 1958. Seeing the handwriting on the wall, Batista fled to the Dominican Republic on Jan. 1, 1959 looting the country's treasury of $300 Million.[2] Castro now controlled the country.

In 1959 Fidel came to the United States, flying into New York at the invitation of the Press Club. He told the American people, "I know what the world thinks of us, that we are Communists and of course I have said very clearly that we are not Communists, very clearly."

Fidel was greeted like a rock star on the streets of New York, even though that term had not yet been coined. Men shook his hand; women hugged and kissed him. He signed autographs, ate hot dogs, and threw a baseball at Yankee Stadium. He made quite an impression with his scruffy beard, his open collar military fatigues and his ever-present cigar.

That image had to cause heartburn to the 'spit and polish' five-star general who occupied the White House, President Dwight (Ike) Eisenhower. Fidel, who had no experience governing, flew to Washington to meet with Ike to seek guidance and assistance from the US government. Ike ignored Castro and went to play golf. Instead he had Vice President Richard Nixon meet with Fidel. This was insulting to Castro who labeled Eisenhower 'the senile golfer in the White House.'

Castro felt he had been blown off by the President of the United States. As a result Castro left Washington and headed home. He then reached out to Moscow and he was warmly received by Premier Nikita Khrushchev. The rest, as the old saying goes, is history. Had Eisenhower taken Castro under his wing and offered assistance in setting up his government, who knows where this situation might have led. Cuba could conceivably have become the 51st State. If Castro had been in the US'

---

2   *wikipedia.org/wiki/Fulgencio_Batista*

corner, the Bay of Pigs and Cuban Missile Crisis would never have occurred.

The Bay of Pigs was a fiasco that took place in April 1961 three months after President Kennedy took office. A Central Intelligence Agency-backed attack on Cuba using Cuban exiles failed miserably and dozens of these exiles were executed and many more taken prisoner. The Missile Crisis took place from Oct. 14-Oct. 28, 1962. After the Bay of Pigs, Khrushchev was able to convince Castro that he needed protection from the US. The Soviet Union began to transfer missiles to Cuba and set up launch bases. After a showdown in which the US and USSR came to the brink of nuclear war, an agreement was reached. The Soviets removed their missiles from Cuba, and the US removed missiles from Turkey and Italy.

Twenty months after the Bay of Pigs and two months after the Missile Crisis, Castro traded 1,113 prisoners captured in the failed Bay of Pigs invasion back to the United States. On Dec. 21, 1962 he accepted $53 Million in food and medicine to repatriate the prisoners. Castro insisted on food and medicine rather than cash. The US government did not have to pony up for this; all the food and medicine were donated by private companies in the United States.[3]

In early 1962 while many Cuban exiles were still being held in Cuba, President Kennedy had signed an executive order on February 8 making the Blockade permanent. He had originally intended to sign it on February 7 but held it up so his Press Secretary Pierre Salinger could go out and buy him a good supply of Cuban cigars. When Salinger showed up at the White House with 1200 Petit H. Upman cigars, JFK signed the order.

This Blockade is the most enduring trade embargo between two countries in history. It was codified in 1992 with the Cuban Democracy Act[4] and tightened in 1996 with the Helm Burton Act.[5] And like the question posed in the introduction, Cubans wonder constantly why do Americans hate them and keep this Blockade

---

3   wikipedia.org/wiki/Bay_of_Pigs_Invasion
4   state.gov/www/regions/wha/cuba/democ_act_1992.html
5   state.gov/www/regions/wha/cuba/helms.html

in place? Their beloved Fidel reminds them constantly that the Blockade is the doing of the 'imperialist norteamericanos' as he refers to Americans. Without the ability to travel there and interact with the Cubans and show them how compassionate we are, Americans will carry this epitaph for many years to come.

For all the bluster and blather that spews from the politicians in South Florida, the Blockade does not hurt Fidel or Raul Castro. They dress well, eat well, are provided excellent healthcare, and are transported in fine automobiles. The same is true for Communist Party leaders. I've watched Raul's motorcade many times from a balcony on the Malecon. And you will read in this book how US products circumvent the Blockade and also how China and Vietnam are willing trade partners with Cuba, shipping billions of dollars of consumer goods to the island.

So why does the Cuban-Floridian delegation in Congress – the 'Miami Cartel' want to keep the Blockade in place? The ones most hurt by it are family members and fellow countrymen back in Cuba. The answer: money, which pours from the US Treasury into the Miami-Cartel financial black hole. Entities such as Radio/TV Marti, Center for a Free Cuba, Directorio Democratico Cubano Inc., Creative Associates, and International Relief and Development among others. These groups get millions of dollars for various outreaches and 'democracy building' programs but they lack any serious accountability. (These groups are explored in depth in Chapter 28)

Included are groups with swollen payrolls and expenses that put little money into programs that touch the Cuban people and whose employees funnel money into the campaign coffers of the Miami Cartel. These people despise the ordinary Cubans on the island because they haven't rebelled and overthrown Castro. This is political corruption and cronyism at its worst, and ironically those who practice it best also are the ones who continually attack Castro and his 'cronies and thugs.'

The US Government also gives grants to various universities to study and design what type of government Cuba should have after the Castros. Why not let the people of Cuba do that, as did the people in all the former Soviet Republics?

5

2. Bienvenido á Cuba

The Blockade restricts direct flights to Cuba from the United States. The only cities currently offering charter flights to Cuba are Miami and Tampa. Of course, access can be had from any city in Canada or Mexico. The Miami flight generally carries Cuban exiles that are going home to visit family. It is difficult though to determine who is truly an exile visiting family and who may be associated with a Miami-based anti-Castro terrorist organization. Hence security is very tight at Miami International Airport as it is at Jose Marti International Airport in Havana.

Jose Marti has a unique process for incoming passengers: all baggage coming off the plane is screened through metal detectors in a back room before being put out onto the baggage carousel.

Passenger carry-on baggage is also screened through metal detectors after passengers clear immigration and make their way to baggage claim. On flights from Cancun or Mexico City there can be many Cuban nationals who are returning with all sorts of personal products: clothing, electronics, automobile parts, appliances. This can delay the screening of passenger luggage considerably. A one to two-hour wait for luggage at Jose Marti Airport is not unusual.

If you are a non-resident and are bringing in a substantial number of items, you will have to wait in the Aduana line with the Cuban nationals. Your first view of Havana outside the terminal may be disappointing. If you are expecting to see the 1950s era cars those are generally in the downtown area. You will, however, be greeted by a very friendly driver with a government owned CubaTaxi, or by prior arrangement a driver with a private car.

Progressing toward downtown Havana, one is stricken by the number of billboards along the roadways, though none are promoting commercial products. All of the billboards have quotes and photos of Cuban heroes: Jose Marti, Edward Maceo, Che Gueverra, Camilo Cienfuegos, and of course the Castro brothers. Many billboards also honor the so-called Five Heroes who are described in Chapter 18.

Central Havana is a large slum-like area with dilapidated buildings, some which collapse on occasion. Many have roofs missing and trees growing through them! If one looks beyond the dilapidation and the grime, many of these building facades are examples of beautiful architecture. Of course, the signature feature of Havana is the Malecon, an 8-kilometer-long seawall which is the social center of Havana life. Families sit along the Malecon during the day, and after dark the Malecon is virtually shoulder-to-shoulder young adults. Cubans are fun-loving and social, and with limited resources they put both those qualities on display on the Malecon at night.

3. The Cuban People

Cuba's No. 1 one crop may be sugar, but its greatest asset is its people. Cubans are the most resourceful people in the world. Cubans were recycling long before the first Earth Day. A cellophane wrapper becomes a grocery sack; an old pair of pants becomes a baby blanket; a twin blade razor becomes an X-acto® knife; old cloth baby diapers become women's sanitary napkins; an odd pipe, metal plate, or other solid object become pieces of an engine or chassis in a 1955 era US automobile.

When you ask the Cubans about their limited resources and their need to be creative, they will reply, "Is Cuba - With American Bloqueo we no have things to buy in stores. Is okay." (SIC) Cubans are leery of criticizing their own government. They fear being overheard by the Secret Police or their neighborhood CDR, Comité Para la Defensa de la Revolución. The Committee for the Defense of the Revolution is a kind of neighborhood watch program, but one that watches out for crimes against the state not property crimes or crimes against persons.

Cubans are warm and friendly once you get past the awkwardness of being behind the 'American Blockade.' Cubans are all about family. Due largely to economic circumstances multiple generations often live together. Whether it's a one-story low-rise building or a six-story multi-unit, each family's home is referred to as their casa or house. There may be grandparents, parents, multiple siblings, some with spouses and children, aunts or uncles all living together.

Most Cuban homes have no running hot water. The cold water comes through a tap in the kitchen as well as one in the bath which are connected to a water tank on the roof. Water trucks replenish the supply in the tanks. A shower is taken by heating water on the stove and then washing with it in a pan in the bathroom. Some homes have electrified shower heads which fast heat the water, but the supply is not always steady.

In spite of limited capabilities and even more limited availability of toiletries, Cubans are very particular about their personal hygiene. In fact, when you walk along the Malecon at night and see the young people they are all well-groomed and neatly dressed. The young ladies are very pretty, and the young men are quite handsome. Many of them are buff from working out in gyms that use old-style weights and some that are created with ingenuity. Gym is a favorite and popular pastime.

Toiletries are limited and costly. One US dollar = .97 CUC. Cubans buy disposable razors on the street for one CUC each. A bar of soap costs two CUC, a tube of toothpaste 3.5 CUC and a woman's sanitary pad costs one CUC. Television access is limited as Cubans have five television channels controlled by state media. Two primarily broadcast news programs, some of which could be considered propaganda. The others offer children's programs and Mexican Telenovelas. Sometimes American programming will come on with movies from one of the HBO channels. With little to watch, many Cubans take advantage of the gym.

Cuban workers are terribly underpaid. The official minimum wage is 10 CUC per month. Most adults work for an average wage of 20 CUC per month. They receive monthly allotments of rice, black beans, and sugar. Mothers of newborn babies are given an allotment of powdered milk until the child turns 7 years old. Cuban housewives sit at their tables socializing with friends while sorting through their rice allotment, picking out small stones and grains of sand.

Some Cubans have perfected the art of the hustle and are referred to as jineteros or street jockeys. Cigars, rum, leather goods, female or male companionship - it's all game in the jinetero world. The usual hustle goes something like this: "Hey my friend, you want some cigars? At the factory they cost $300 a box. My cousin he works in the factory and he steals the cigar in his pants. At night he goes home and put them in a box and sells the box for $150. Very good price." (SIC)

Many Cuban young ladies seek to leave the country via a marriage license. Some have married Spaniards, Italians, Germans and other Europeans or Latin Americans. But the gold standard for these girls is an American man. Girls as young as 19 years old will propose marriage to men up to middle-age! These girls are well versed in the I-130 and I-129F US government forms which are applications for a visa for an alien spouse and alien fiancé, respectively. They will bring their parents out to meet a potential husband and the parents will help intensify the sales pitch. In church they may even bring the priest in on the discussion!

Regrettably, with low wages and high prices for many consumer items in Cuba, many young people turn to the sex trade to augment their income. This has become well-known across Europe and European tourists travel to Cuba to take advantage of these young ladies and men.

If there is at least a minor consolation in this sex trade it is that there are no minors involved like in Southeast Asia, and it pretty much takes place on the street or along the Malecon in one-on-one encounters. Long gone are the brothels of the dictator Batista and his US Mafia associates. Young men or women who negotiate an encounter cannot go to the tourists' hotel rooms without the tourist having to pay a double occupancy upcharge and the Cuban national having to register as a guest with their National ID Card.

Hence, these encounters are facilitated in 'casa particulars' or private guest houses. While these generally rent for $25 a night per bedroom for tourists, an owner often will rent it by the hour for a liaison. Contrary to the criticism that the government does nothing to police the sex trade and therefore is no better than the Batista dictatorship, there is in fact a major difference. Under Batista's rule the American Mafia had brothels all over the country protected by his Interior Ministry, where men went to consort with young girls, some who were underage and who'd been kidnapped from their families, many while walking home from school. Like all prostitution the money went to the Mafia and the girls were likely paid a token if at all. At the end of 1958 it was estimated that 11,500 females worked as prostitutes under Batista and the US Mafia.[6]

The current sex trade is difficult to police because most encounters are negotiated in private one-on-one conversations. However, police will stop a young male or female they see walking with an older foreigner and determine the relationship. If a liaison does take place however, the Cuban has the security of utilizing a casa particular with the client where the owner likely has a very sharp machete in case things get out of hand.

The biggest difference between this sex trade and the prostitution in the Batista era is what is driving it. In the Batista era, it was an industry controlled by the US Mafia who paid kickbacks to Batista whose Interior Ministry helped provide young girls. Young people in Cuba today do not work the streets regularly or hang around a brothel seeking tricks. They may only have a liaison one, two, or three nights in a month. These liaisons generally are objective driven; the money is to help their family with household expenses, purchase new clothes, procure a cell phone, buy shoes, or even as one young man who I met was doing - raising 600 CUC to pay for his wedding.

He did not want his fiancé working for the money so he took to raising it himself. He stashed the currency in an empty rum bottle so it could not be misused. As he approached his goal, a new friend helped him round off the 600 CUC, and he and his fiancé smashed the bottle and were married four weeks later.

In Cuba, sex is both a currency and a commodity. When someone is treated well – given toiletries, taken to a fine restaurant, offered a bus ticket on the upscale Viazul inter-city bus rather

---

6   *historyofcuba.com/history/time/timetbl3b.htm*

than the Astro line, the retort is generally 'do you want [sex] for this?'

This is not to excuse the sex trade in Cuba. But it illustrates how desperate financial predicaments can push people to do things that run counter to their own moral beliefs. Many in the US government – especially the Miami Cartel – would blame this on the Cuban government.

While the Cuban government does bear some of the blame so too does the United States government. For 54 year, the US has kept its foot on the throat of the Cuban people. God only knows what changes might have come to Cuba had Americans been able to travel there freely and do business there for the past half-century.

In 2011, Senator Bob Menendez (D-NJ) made a speech on the floor of the US Senate. He cited the fact that Voyeur Magazine (Inflight Magazine of Virgin Airlines?) cited Cuba as the No. 1 hotspot for sex travel in the world.[7] Considering the reputation of Thailand and Singapore that claim would seem to be a real stretch.

Menendez is a classic politician of Cuban heritage: bloviating about a situation and blaming Fidel Castro while not acknowledging the true cause of the problem. How a politician who claims the moral ground can be so heartless to his fellow countrymen is impossible to grasp.

---

7   *Congressional Record-2009-03-02-pt1-Page S2613*

4. People-to-People Programs

When President Obama relaxed the rules for travel to Cuba in 2009, he cited his desire to expand People-to-People programs. The White House press release of Jan. 14, 2011 stated, "These measures will increase people-to-people contact; support civil society in Cuba; enhance the free flow of information to, from, and among the Cuban people; and help promote their independence from Cuban authorities."

Purposeful People-to-People programs are designed to foster good will and dialogue between groups of Americans and Cubans of various backgrounds and stature. In theory it sounds good, but from the American perspective it is very limited.

Licensed People-to-People travel is limited. Activities typical of visiting tourists are prohibited. Organized escorted groups, academic groups, religious groups, trade missions, and journalists are permitted to travel. These programs are great in theory, but have a major shortcoming. Those who travel under this program are generally on a tight schedule arranged by the Cuban government therefore the amount of time to wander freely and interact with the Cuban people is limited.

One such trip was undertaken in March 2012 by a group of students from Bentley University in Waltham, Massachusetts under the direction of World History Professor Cyrus Veeser.

The group was in Cuba during their spring break week. They began their week in Havana meeting with tourism officials and representatives of the School of Tourism at the University of Havana. Next they traveled to the city of Trinidad for several days to observe the resort operations at hotels built in partnership with the Cuban government.

On their return to Havana, they had a brief opportunity to meet with an ordinary Cuban. The students invited this person to share a meal, giving them the opportunity to inquire about basic life in Cuba, about the geography of the island, and about the educational system, including free university tuition. The Bentley students said that was the best portion of their trip.

One student said: "It was amazing, especially the time we had with this person. He is a really great guy. It was calm and relaxed and he answered our questions about everyday life. He spent time with us at the university and then he joined us for dinner."

People-to-People programs give groups the opportunity to learn about the Cuban homeland but it also lacks in affording Cubans the ability to learn about the Americans' homeland. With the technology that exists in 2012 that kind of exchange of cultural information should take place via the internet. But with the government restricting internet access in Cuba, only by personal travel can attitudes change. If Americans were free to visit Cuba at their own will and to interact with the Cuban people at their own will, this could help change attitudes about the US and the mindset of the Cubans.

On Dec. 15, 2011 US Senator Marco Rubio (R-FL) went on a tirade on the Senate floor against People-to-People programs, reading the itineraries of several groups that included salsa dancing in the evening.[8] Like all other Miami Cartel politicians, Senator Rubio rehashed the 54- year-old worthless argument that this puts 'millions of dollars' into the hands of the Castro government. Seriously Senator Rubio, millions of dollars put into the Cuban economy by a few thousand travelers?

Many Cubans loathe Americans because of people like Senator Marco Rubio: a Cuban-Floridian who for years lied about his

---

8   *Congressional Record-2011-12-15-pt1-Pg S8671*

family history and in so doing continually trashed his family's homeland. He told those lies to cozy up to the Banana Republic of South Florida to develop his political career. Like his mentor House Foreign Affairs Committee Chairman Congressman Ileana Ros-Lehtinen (R-FL) and the Diaz-Balart political clan, Rubio is widely despised by ordinary Cubans. They see him as a political opportunist and would not be sad to see his demise.

Another point in Rubio's rant on the Senate floor was that one itinerary included a visit to the Moncada Barracks in Santiago de Cuba. This is the location where on July 26, 1953, Fidel Castro and 100 rebels launched their revolution. The Moncada Barracks is the Cuban equivalent of the Village Green in Lexington where on April 19, 1775 the 'shot heard 'round the world' was fired.

Rubio's rant and expression of disgust over Cubans sharing their heritage with American visitors is emblematic of the mind-set that exists with the Miami Cartel. They claim to want freedom for their homeland, but in reality they want to take over the country and wipe out any memory of Fidel Castro. Even in Vietnam one of the most popular tourist destinations is a portion of the former 'Hanoi Hilton' prisoner of war camp as it is part of Vietnam's history. Rubio also routinely makes the false claim that Cubans are not allowed to be on the beaches. Any lie is appropriate I guess if it makes the crowd gasp. Senator, I have observed thousands of Cubans enjoying themselves on the beaches of both the north and south shores. Perhaps you should visit your father's homeland sometime so that you can see the truth and retire the tall tales.

Does Senator Rubio expect People-to-People travelers to sit in their hotel rooms at night and stare at the walls? That surely isn't how Congressmen and Senators spend their free time when they travel around the world on so-called fact-finding junkets. So if participants in People-to-People travel participate in social activities with Cuban citizens it can be considered off-setting all of the vitriol directed at Cuba through the years by bloviating politicians. What exactly is wrong with that, Senator Rubio? You and the rest of the Miami Cartel in Congress have done a great deal of damage that needs to be countered. Cubans need to see that average Americans are not as morally shallow as the Miami Cartel. This is People-to-People social interaction at its finest.

After the departure from Cuba of Pope Benedict in March 2012 a group of volunteers celebrated with a pig roast and salsa dancing. Even some religious participated in the dancing. Should an American volunteer present have sat the evening out to appease Senator Rubio? Socializing and interacting with Cuban hosts can be very rewarding – for both sides.

In February, 2013 Senator Rubio gave a speech to an anti-Castro political group. He proclaimed, "Cuba is not a zoo, where you get to pay for admission and watch people living in cages."[9] Well, Senator Rubio since you've never been there please allow me to educate you. Cuba is a zoo with people living in sub-par conditions behind a fence that the Miami Cartel and terrorists like your mentor Ileana Ros-Lehtinen[10] have constructed to hem them in, refusing to allow them to freely travel to the US or be visited by American tourists.

9   nbclatino.com/2013/03/13/senator-rubio-slams-cuba-travel-cuba-is-not-a-zoo-senator-leahy-fires-back/
10   *President George W. Bush in the War on Terror proclaimed in 2003 "If you support a terrorist, you're a terrorist." Ileana Ros-Lehtinen has given aid and comfort and support to multiple terrorists*

5. Cuba's Beauty and Its Tourist Potential

No tourists spend like American tourists. You can literally take that statement to the bank. Cuba has a plethora of locations that would be of interest to tourists. Beach activities, flora and fauna, mountain hiking, architecture, churches and religious sites, Trinidad, Old Havana, and the Malecon would appeal to visitors.

El Nicho – the niche – in Cienfuegos province, has spectacular mountain waterfalls (cascadas) and rivers where swimming is a delight. The area has the feel of a tropical rain forest. A cottage industry could be created in these hills with zip-lines and mountain biking accommodating tourists. There also are cascadas located about a 90-mile drive west of Havana. While not as expansive as El Nicho, they are beautiful and refreshing nevertheless.

Cuba's beaches have spectacular white sand, sparkling blue water, and the daiquiris, mojitos, and Cuba Libres are reputed to flow freely. The majority of the beaches are on the north side of the island in Varadero, a 22km long isthmus, a ¼ mile wide, with a 15km long beach, and they all are worth a five-star rating. The beaches have all-inclusive hotels which are attractive and very moderately priced. A double room in September (hurricane season) would run about $52 per night while a double room in January would run $98 per night. Tourist hotels have more expansive television access, including HBO, ESPN, CNN, and Canadian and Chinese channels.

Portions of Old Havana have restored buildings with unique architecture, but the most highly-regarded city in Cuba for architecture is Trinidad along the south coast. Not only does Trinidad have exquisite and well-maintained architecture, but it has two beautiful beaches nearby.

The area best known for its mountains, rivers, thick forests, and scenery is Oriente, or the Eastern end of the island by Santiago de Cuba Province. El Cobre is the home of the cathedral which houses the statue of Nuestra Senora de la Caridid del Cobre, the Patroness of Cuba.

In 1612 this statue of the Virgin Mary holding the baby Jesus was found floating in the bay.[11] It is housed in the cathedral which includes a repository of letters, braces, crutches, locks of hair, medals, and other objects left by people who believe their prayers were answered by the Virgin. Among the many testaments is Ernest Hemingway's Pulitzer Prize. University students who felt their prayers were answered in completing their thesis have left their theses with the Virgin.

Cuba is home to many beautiful and ornate Catholic cathedrals and churches. They were boarded up in the 1960's when religion was banned and then reopened in the last 1980's when religion was once again allowed to be practiced. Many have stunning gold leaf around their altar.

All areas of Cuba are easy to access and visit because Cuba has an excellent cross-island tourist transportation network with well-appointed motor coaches acquired from China's Yutong Manufacturing. Private car owners also can be hired at rates less than the government taxi service. Tourists would enjoy interacting with Cubans and learning what wonderful people they are.

---

11   marypages.com/LadyCaridadDelCobre.htm

6. Guantanamo Bay (Gitmo)

The US Naval Base at Guantanamo Bay is the oldest US military installation outside the United States proper. First discovered by Christopher Columbus on his second trip to the New World, he named it Puerto Grande or Great Port. On June 10, 1898, US Marines landed there during the Spanish-American War. The US has controlled the property ever since. In 1903, President Teddy Roosevelt negotiated a lease with the Cuban government for the bay for 2,000 gold coins per year.

In 1934, the lease was renegotiated by the Franklin Delano Roosevelt administration with the government led by Fulgencio Batista. The annual lease payment was raised to $4,085.

When Castro's revolution was successful in overthrowing Batista in 1959, the Castro government demanded that the bay be returned. The US refused the request. Since that time, the Cuban government has cashed only one rent check, the very first it received, and cashed it due to confusion. Every subsequent check through the present sits in a drawer in Havana not cashed. The United States argues that cashing that one check signified the Castro government's ratification of the lease. Havana, of course, sees it differently.[12]

---

12   *marypages.com/LadyCaridadDelCobre.htm*

7. Communication – Telecom and Internet

I f Cuba is a World-Class country with a Third World mindset, then its communications capabilities are Fourth World, if there is such a thing. The only word that can be used to describe Cuba's on-island as well as its international telecommunications capabilities is *horrendous*. ETECSA is the military-owned telephone company, 27percent of which is owned by Telecomm Italia.

Few private homes have telephones, thus people are forced to use public telephones attached to the outside of buildings. In some cases they compete with traffic, barking dogs, crowing roosters, etc. to hear the other party.

These public telephones require the use of a pre-paid telephone calling card. There are little booths scattered across the country about the size of a one-car garage. Cubans have to stand in line, sometimes for as long as 20 minutes to put minutes on their calling card. The transaction must be in cash and in person.

Once the card is charged up and an individual wants to make a telephone call, he has to go to a public phone. If he is unlucky, the two phones per location are occupied by others, and he has to wait. The only limitation on how long a person may use a telephone is based on the number of minutes he has on his card.

When a caller does get an available telephone, he or she has to deal with another conversation going on about three feet away on the other phone. This makes it very difficult for individuals discussing confidential family or work information or having an intimate conversation.

While they were illegal until 2008, many Cubans are now in possession of mobile phones. Cubans who have received them as gifts from family members or friends or who engaged in the sex trade to afford to buy one enjoy the 'convenience' of cellular phones. The cost for a minute of talk on a Cubacel (Subsidiary of ETECSA) is approximately 49 cents.

How does someone earning less than $20 per month afford to load pre-paid minutes onto their cellphone? (Note how everything in Cuba is prepaid) They reach out to family, friends, and acquaintances in the US to 'top up' their telephone with minutes. There are several US-based vendors that can be utilized to add minutes to a Cuban cell phone and they frequently offer a two-for-one promotion so the Cubans can get double credit.

As for Internet service, Cubans should be so fortunate as to have the 'speed and reliability' that Americans had 20 years ago with dial-up. Cuba's Internet service is also operated by ETECSA, a subsidiary of the Cuban military and access is relayed slowly by satellite.

The Internet goes down frequently, sometimes for hours at a time. Here again pre-pay is the mode of access. Just as Cubans stand in line to add minutes to their telephone calling card, they also must stand in line to purchase Internet access cards.

Each card gives them 30 minutes access to the Internet and costs three CUC. Waiting in line to purchase the card is a minor inconvenience compared to waiting to use a computer workstation at an Internet center. Each Internet center has 30 or so workstations. Whether you walk by in the morning, afternoon, or evening, every workstation is occupied and there are 20-30 individuals milling about outside waiting for someone to vacate a workstation. People do not form lines, so you have to go around asking to determine who was the last person before you to show up.

When a workstation does come available, the bandwidth is so limited that the PC runs very slowly. (A computer at an upscale hotel took eight minutes to download the front page of Facebook) Users have limited access to printers and many Web pages including You Tube™, Wikipedia, and Skype™ are blocked by the government. The worst nightmare is when a user is in the midst of an operation and his 30-minute card runs out. The PC just shuts down and all is lost.

Internet service in one's home is available in Cuba at a cost of 70 CUC per month, only after the applicant is approved by ETECSA as not being subversive. Less than 3 percent of the Cuban population has this type of Internet access.

Many individuals who have home internet access have become entrepreneurs of sorts as they allow their neighbors to use their computers to access the internet at rates of about one CUC for 20 minutes. The benefit to users is not only financial, but the entrepreneur's computer does not shut down at the end of 30 minutes unless of course there is routine downtime. They also charge neighbors a fee to have an email account, and these are tied to the owner's original account.

Foreign visitors can use Internet services for a fee at hotels. Sometimes this could mean a walk of a mile or more. The best internet service on the island is the Nacional Hotel in Havana where all foreign dignitaries stay, but even it does not come close to DSL.

Cubans' hopes for faster and more reliable internet service were raised back in 2009. A Miami-based company called TeleCuba was granted a license by the US Treasury Department to lay a 110-mile cable from Key West, Fla., to Cuba, an investment of $18 Million.[13] The Cuban government did not approve the TeleCuba deal and instead chose to deal with Alba, a consortium run by the late Hugo Chavez's Venezuelan government. The cable was projected to be 1,000 miles long and run at a cost of $70 Million.[14]

Installation of the cable began from Venezuela in January 2011 and was touted in the state-run Cuban media for several months and its July 2011 launch was predicted as the era when

---

13   telecuba.com/pressrelease_nov102010.htm

14   bnamericas.com/news/telecommunications/work-begins-on-alba-submarine-cable

Cuba would propel itself into the world economy in spite of the US Blockade. Suddenly all mention of the fiber optic cable ceased. Not a word was broadcast on state TV or printed in the state-run newspaper Granma. Almost three years after the projected start-up date, the old slow satellite internet service is still in place. Ordinary Cubans on the street will tell you that rumor has it that sharks devoured the cable underwater.

Individuals who work in state-run companies become exasperated when their Internet shuts down or is turned off for the day. How does Cuba expect to advance itself in the world economy when its functionaries and workers receive email messages long after they have been sent or have to wait hours for attachments to download?

In May, 2012, the Venezuelan science and technology minister Jorge Arreaza told reporters the cable is absolutely operational.[15] "It will depend on Cuba's government how it uses it...but we know that the undersea cable is in full operation." Arreaza intimated that the Venezuelan government has used the cable to connect beyond Cuba.

It is probably very likely that this cable was used for communications during the various extended stays that Chavez spent receiving medical treatment in Cuba before he died.

In the fall of 2011 at a conference on social media, Cuban Foreign Minister Bruno Rodriguez warned of the danger of the Internet and alluded how it helped bring about the downfall of governments in Libya and Egypt. The internet did not bring down Libya and Egypt. Corrupt leaders who violated the basic rights of their people brought down those governments. Rodriguez stated, "The euphoria around social networks coexists with the risk of regime change operations, which have increased, as well as the threat to peace. These hazardous conditions make it necessary and urgent that we appropriate these platforms."[16]

Might this explain the delay in service? Could the government fear a Cuban Spring if communications were facilitated across the island? One should consider that Castro and Che did

---

15   miamiherald.com/2012/05/25/v-print/2817534/fiber-optic-cable-benefiting-only.html
16   havanatimes.org/?p=56922

not have the internet in the 1950s yet they were successful at replacing a corrupt government. In establishing his education program in the early 1960s Fidel Castro's goal was educational parity with the US. He achieved a higher literacy rate than the US, but literacy no longer means just reading and writing. By depriving broad use of the Internet, a vast chasm will develop between the technological literacy of young people of the two countries. As Fidel Castro is in the twilight of his life, his greatest legacy of educational excellence is fading as well, as his people are being dumbed down.

If the government continues to restrict Cubans' access to the Internet and communications then what the Cuban people will need is the tourist-net; face-to-face interactions with foreigners. Cubans would certainly appreciate the opportunity to communicate with people from outside their country, especially those from the United States if the travel ban were lifted.

8. Looking After the Folks Back Home

Under the Bush Administration, the family-visit policy – driven by the Miami Mafia – limited Cuban-Americans to one visit to family in Cuba every three years. Talk about family values. President Obama removed that restriction to allow for unlimited travel by Cuban-Americans.

When it comes to Cuban-Americans staying in touch with family and friends in Cuba, the situation is quite bad. Exorbitant telephone rates make calling to the island prohibitive. Below is a cross section of countries and per minute rates to call there from the US:

Country	US cents
Antarctica	45.0
Dominican Republic	9.9
Guatemala	11.9
Iran	7.9
Lebanon	21.0
Netherlands Antilles	12.9
North Korea	99.0
Saint Kitts and Nevis	24.9
South Korea	3.9
Syria	21.9
Yemen	18.9
CUBA	**89.9**

All rates are for calls to cell phones from the United States using Rebtel.com

So we see how Cuban exiles in the US get shaken down financially trying to call family in Cuba. One can call anywhere in the Caribbean for much less. Call Iran, Syria, or Yemen – terrorist states - and it's much cheaper. The only calls that cost more than Cuba are to North Korea, but using a cell phone in North Korea is now a war crime punishable by death so that's a moot point.

Sending cash remittances to relatives or friends in Cuba cost 10 percent per transaction via Western Union, the sole transfer agent. Remittances were limited and severely restricted under the Bush administration. In 2009, President Obama eliminated the monetary limit for family remittances and also now allows for remittances of up to $500 per quarter to non-family members. Undocumented Mexicans, Guatemalans, or Hondurans who are here in the US working can send home unlimited funds and pay a mere $3.99 to send up to $3000.

In the speech by Senator Menendez mentioned earlier, Menendez also tore into the Castro regime for taking 10 percent of the remittance amount. That practice stopped years ago, but it makes for good political bloviating. It is curious that Menendez never criticized Western Union for taking a 10 percent fee from the senders here in the US.

Gift packs can be sent to Cuba via US mail, but are limited to 4 pounds and a value of $800. Anyone who would put $800 worth of merchandise in a 4-pound box likely runs a very good chance that the package will disappear once it hits the island. Regardless of the value of the package, the odds of it making it to its intended recipient in three to four weeks are rather slim. The Bush administration had placed an embargo on shipping soap or shampoo to family members – suggesting that the Cuban government provide those items to its citizens. Acting like grown-ups, the Obama administration lifted this ban.

There are several private shipping firms in South Florida that will ship packages of virtually any size to Cuba. Delivery takes about two weeks. A 17-pound package shipped via a private shipper cost $162 and took 16 days to arrive at its destination. By contrast, 17-pound boxes shipped to the Dominican Republic or Cancun, Mexico, by either UPS or FedEx ship for 2/3 of the cost and arrive in two days. Regrettably, neither UPS nor FedEx can do business in Cuba because of the Blockade.

Opening up the country to these two shipping companies would facilitate the shipping of products, goods, housewares, and clothing to families in Cuba by family members in the US.

In July 2012 a new start-up company, International Port Corporation, began accepting shipments to Cuba from its Miami operation. And did the chair of the House Committee on Foreign Affairs, Ileana Ros-Lehtinen, applaud this new inexpensive service designed to aid both her constituents in South Florida and the people of her homeland? No. She launched an investigation into whether IPC had the appropriate government licenses.

Expanding shipping options would greatly help improve the quality of life for people in Cuba which they so desperately deserve.

9. Cuban Foreign Ministry (MINREX)

In January 2012, volunteer groups were working toward the celebration of two Liturgies to be celebrated by Pope Benedict XVI in March. An American citizen assisting the effort pondered ways the Cuban government might leverage the Pope's visit to bring the US Blockade to the attention of the American people via media that would be covering the Papal visit.

Several ideas were put in writing and this citizen convinced a Cuban associate to accompany him to the Cuban Foreign Ministry (Known as MinRex)[17] to present his white paper for consideration. He carried the four- page document in a manila folder and hoped to visit with a responsible person who could seriously evaluate the enclosed ideas.

Two soldiers with side arms stood outside the MinRex building, and after the associate explained why they had come the two were waived inside. An explanation of intent was then given to a security agent in the lobby who then waived the duo to the receptionist desk. There were no metal detectors entering the building, only security cameras in the reception area.

The Cuban associate spoke to three people on the telephone and then hung up. He announced to the American that some-

---

17   *cubaminrex.cu/english/Ministry/ministry.htm*

one would be down to meet with them shortly. The person who arrived was a senior staffer within the North America division.

To put this in context that US readers can relate to, this would be like approaching the front door of the US State Department and saying, "Hi, I'd like to meet with one of Secretary John Kerry's senior staff members and I want to share this document here in this folder. It has ideas about how to deal with President Kim Jung Un in North Korea."

Such a foray would probably end at the metal detectors, the folder and document would likely be confiscated and bagged then evaluated for anthrax. Meanwhile the individual would probably be questioned, finger-printed and God knows what else.

This Cuban government staffer could not have been more gracious. She first spoke with the Cuban associate in Spanish; then turned to the American and spoke in perfect English. Learning he was from Texas, she inquired as to what he thought Rick Perry's chances were in the GOP primaries. On several occasions the American tried graciously to dismiss himself so she could get back to her work, stating that all the details were in the document, but she wanted to hear all the details first hand. At the end of the meeting she asked if the duo would wait while she went back to her office on an upper floor to get business cards to give to her visitors.

Ultimately a variation of one of the suggestions was implemented, but not in a way that had anything to do with the Blockade. The suggestion that large building-sized banners be displayed by the Place de la Revolucion during the Papal Mass in Havana was adopted with variations.

One banner which hung on the building with Che Guevara face on the front was an eight-story-long Cuban flag. The other on the facade of the Interior Ministry building was a banner 10 stories long and even wider with a depiction of Nuestra Señora de la Caridad del Cobre, the Patroness of Cuba whose 400th anniversary the Holy Father had come to celebrate.

The underlying point of this book is driven home in this anecdote. The fact that *one of Fidel's thugs* as the Miami Cartel refers to Cuban government staffers, could not have been more pleasant, accommodating, and open to suggestions from a norteamericano.

That really should come as no surprise because Cubans are wonderful, friendly people.

Pope Benedict XVI welcomed at Santiago de Cuba by President Raul Castro

I am proud to have inspired this banner at Pope Benedict's Mass in Havana on March 28, 2012. It hung from the Interior Ministry HQ

10. Fidel and His People

El Comandante. El Jefe. Enigma. Dichotomy. Evil. Wily. Brutal. Survivor. Dictator. Grandfather. There have been many labels attached to Fidel Castro through the years. Castro held power from 1959 to 2006 when he handed over power to his brother Raul. He outlasted 10 US presidents.

There is one other label that is frequently attached to Fidel, but it's only heard in Cuba: *beloved*. Yes, Cuban people may be frustrated with their situation but for anyone under the age of 54, they have spent their entire life hearing from Fidel Castro that their plight is the fault of the Americans. The enduring travel ban has reinforced that gospel because the Cuban people have not had the opportunity to interact with Americans on their streets, along their Malecon, or in their cafes.

Hence, the Cuban man on the street believes that the Americans are the bogeyman. Fidel, to use an old expression, 'has kept the trains running on time,' therefore he is their hero. With Fidel as protagonist in this long one-act play, along have come dozens of characters in the Miami Cartel who have verbally trashed him at every chance. Cuban state-media takes these characters' words and turns them into a positive for Castro earning him the support and empathy of his people.

It's easy for Cuban state-media to do this with the human cartoon character who for several years chaired the House Foreign Relations Committee, terrorist collaborator Ileana Ros-Lehtinen. She's the daughter of an old Batistani. In an interview for a British documentary about Castro in 2006 she stated, "I would welcome the opportunity to have anyone assassinate Fidel Castro."[18]

When the clip aired she claimed her remarks were spliced together and threatened to sue, so the documentarians released the entire interview which showed no splicing had taken place. (More on Ros-Lehtinen in Chapter 32)

Chalk one up for Fidel. Ileana Ros-Lehtinen became more reviled than before by the Cuban people for stating what was interpreted as a solicitation for an assassination of Castro. And Fidel became even more beloved.

An informal survey of 50 Cubans between the ages of 19 and 28 along the Malecon one evening in October 2012[19] produced the following results in reply to the question: If you could meet and have dinner with anyone living or deceased, who would you choose:

Fidel Castro	24
Che Guevara	13
One of the Cuban Five	9
Deceased Relative	4

Would American youth answer in similar fashion, naming political figures, or would they skew to sports or pop culture figures? Through 12 years of school Cuban children are constantly taught about their country's heroes. All public buildings in Cuba are named after heroes. Heroes' pictures and their quotes are on billboards around the country. And the No. 1 hero in the country is their beloved El Commandante Fidel Castro.

.

When I was first admitted to CIREN in September 2012 for treatment of Alzheimer's, I had a nurse assigned to my house who was black. She was a lovely human being and we made an instant connection. We talked briefly about life in Cuba in general

---

18 archive.newsmax.com/archives/ic/2006/12/23/220652.shtml?s=ic
19 March 30, 2012 street polling on Malecon; Paul LeBon

and under Fidel. She said to me: "Paul, do you see the color of my skin? I am black. Before Fidel I would never have been able to go to school and become a nurse. Many in my family have received a good education and have important jobs. None of this would have been possible under Batista." The current population breakdown in Cuba is 65% white and the remainder a mix of Black and Mulatta. If you walk through Little Havana in Miami today there are very few Blacks, as the old habits followed.

I also heard first hand from a woman in her 70s about the atrocities against young girls by Batista's Interior Ministry where they would be snatched off the street and forced to work in a brothel for the American Mafia. "Batista and his demons can burn in hell. Thank God for Fidel," she said. Her story, told to me over 2 hours, left me in tears.

In 1961, Fidel Castro sent teachers out into the countryside to teach peasants how to read and write. There is deep seeded love and gratitude for this man, which the Miami Cartel and consequently US officials refuse to acknowledge.

I was in Havana on a humanitarian mission in February 2013. On Feb. 23 the Cuban National Assembly convened its session. A guest speaker was a frail Fidel Castro who spoke for 20 minutes. This was broadcast on national TV. I was returning from the Cathedral of Havana. As I walked along Calle Zanja and Avenida Belascoin, I saw people in restaurants, shops, and homes, watching with tears in their eyes. Cubans adore their hero and leader, and all the ranting and raving on Radio Marti, along Calle Ocho in Miami, or in the halls of Congress by the Miami Cartel will never change that.

11. Cuba's Propaganda Machine

If Cuba does one thing well, it develops great propaganda. The official newspaper *Granma* publishes some pretty amazing articles. It constantly praised Hugo Chavez as a champion of the people, a tireless fighter against oppression and tyranny. It reported his comings and goings to Cuba for cancer treatment and dedicated eight pages to his legacy when he died early in 2013.

Granma also heaps praise on Iranian President Mahmoud Ahmadinejad. He was in Cuba in January 2012 to receive an honorary degree at the University of Havana and this writer came within 60 feet of him. *Granma* reports on the Syrian conflict and claims that President Assad is bombing terrorists bent on destroying the government. Of course they are referring to the bombing of insurgents that has been condemned by the entire free world. Granma blamed the massacre by Assad's troops of over 100 people including 42 children on the Syrian insurgents.

Cuban State TV is not much better. In fall 2011 it repeatedly ran a CNN news piece on the number of Americans who had fallen below the poverty line. (46 Million)[20] One Cuban woman threw that report in the face of an American and she was informed about what had been deleted from the piece: what the actual

20   *money.cnn.com/2011/09/13/news/economy/poverty_rate_income/index.htm*

poverty line was. When she learned it was $24,000 annually for a family of four the woman whose income is less that $20 a month had a change of attitude.

Another favorite of State TV is news clips of American servicemen in the Middle East, sometimes engaging in bad behavior. But all the video of American GIs and Marines may be having a detrimental effect. Last fall two Cuban nationals said about the US service members: "They have all that equipment to fight with and protect themselves. And they are large, larger than us. I hope the US never attacks Cuba."

One person can only nullify so much propaganda in addition to conducting mission activities. But tens of thousands of US tourists, especially young people engaging Cuba's young people, could really make a difference in opening eyes on the island. The US just needs a rational leader who will show the courage to stand up to the Miami Cartel and lift the outdated and ineffective travel ban.

Cubadebate.com is the Cuban government's online propaganda tool. It has more than 89,981 Facebook friends. There are a mere 130 Likes for Radio/TV Marti the Miami Cartel's propaganda tool though no one in Cuba hears it.

12. Pea-brained Diplomacy & Propaganda American Style

In what has been one of the low points of bilateral relations between the U.S. and Cuba in the 21st Century, in 2006 the Bush administration suspended a 25-foot-long electronic ticker billboard on the side of the US Interests Section headquarters in Havana.

The building sits on a curve of the Malecon where cars and buses speed by at 50+ miles per hour. The sign's purpose was to run messages quoting U.S. leaders such as Martin Luther King and Abraham Lincoln to hopefully be viewed by those in transit. The board also ran messages trashing the Cuban government and Fidel Castro.

Fidel Castro put a quick stop to that exposure. He erected more than 100 flag poles in a large square plaza in front of the building and with the flags flapping in the ocean wind the sign was no longer visible. In 2009 the Obama administration put an end to the Bush administration's Times Square on the Malecon.

U.S. diplomats in Cuba are restricted to travel within a 25-mile radius of the Interests Section. Where on earth did the Cubans come up with such an idea? They copied the Americans who had set the same constraint on Cuban diplomats in Washington and New York.

While anonymous Islamist fundamentalists quietly roam the United States seeking targets for terrorism such as the Boston Marathon, credentialed diplomats representing a country which has never engaged in any act of aggression or terrorism against us are treated like the family pet – contained in a limited area.

Worse yet, our diplomats in Cuba who could be visiting the country from Pinar del Rio in the west to Oriente in the east and getting to know the Cuban people, are equally hamstrung.

The Cubans have a large advantage. The United States is an open society with freedom of speech and freedom of the press. So Cuban diplomats in the US are well aware of what is happening in our country and our government. They just have to watch the news and Sunday talk shows. US diplomats have to rely on 'intelligence' supposedly relayed by the various groups within the Miami Cartel, groups who put self-preservation ahead of the interests of the Cuban people.

When the Bush Administration installed a ticker sign on the US Interests Building which ran messages trashing Fidel Castro, Castro erected over 100 flags to block the sign from view. The Obama Administration removed the sign.

13. The U.S. Blockade: Economic Error and a Leaky Bucket

The Cuban Blockade began as a military embargo against the Batista Regime while it gave support to the 26th of July Movement under Fidel Castro. President Kennedy made it permanent on Feb. 8, 1962 one day after his press secretary procured 1,200 Cuban cigars for him. For 30 years, the ability to modify or remove the Blockade rested solely with the president.

In 1992 after 30 years of failed policy, the US Congress decided to make the rules more insidious. The Cuban Democracy Act was passed in Congress and codified the Blockade, giving Congress power over much of it. In 1996, the Helms-Burton Act was passed. Named for Congress' two most rabid anti-Communists trapped in the past, it set restrictions on giving any aid to a future Cuban government unless it met certain benchmarks. It also muddied the waters because it opened a Pandora's Box with respect to individuals who left Cuba voluntarily in the early days of the Revolution, granting them the right to sue for reparations for property they abandoned.

Helms-Burton also raised the ire of much of the world community by making it illegal for any foreign company doing business in Cuba to do business in the United States. Like all GOP legislation the bill was written by lawyers, in this case those representing Bacardi Rum. The law came to be known as the 'Bacardi Law' by opponents.[21]

Visit the Port of Mariel and it looks very different from the news clips of the Mariel boatlift of 1980. This deep water port has state-of-the-art ship and rail accommodations to offload and distribute Chinese goods arriving on container ships. Cubans hate the quality of Chinese products.

So what impact has the US Blockade had on the Cuban economy, correct that – *on the US economy*? In 2006, Cuba purchased 100 locomotives from China. Imagine going to a manufacturer 12,000 miles away when manufacturers are within 1,000 miles. How many jobs might have been created if GE had sold the locomotives?

In 2006, Cuba also purchased 2,500 buses – city buses, plain coaches, and luxury motorcoaches in several sizes to support the tourism industry. These were purchased from Yutong Manufacturing in China. Surely those coaches could have been built by several manufacturers in the United States producing good blue collar jobs for middle-class Americans. Cuba also has purchased 30,000 energy-efficient refrigerators from China and sold them to families for $3. The problem is, they work poorly, forcing residents to put bottled water in the freezer to keep it cold. What a shot in the arm this could have been to the US economy. Lest anyone think that Cuba buys strictly from China, there are two very prominent items that are purchased from Iran and Canada.

In 2007, the Cuban government purchased 200 passenger and 550 freight rail cars from Iran. Surely the freight cars could have been built by Trinity Industries in Dallas. That would have been a great job stimulator as well as a nice addition to Trinity's bottom line. There is no doubt that there are American manufacturers capable of building the 200 passenger cars. Cuba does buy American made rolling stock. However, the yellow school buses with nameplates such as Blue Bird, Thomas, and Wayne that ply the streets of Havana and other cities were bought used from Canada.

Which American products pass through the leaky Blockade Bucket? Coca Cola, Sprite, Fanta, Dell and Acer Computers,

---

21   *library.thinkquest.org/18355/the_helms-burton_act.html*

Microsoft Windows and Office applications, Nabisco cookies, Pringles Potato Chips, Mars bars, Zero bars, Reese's Peanut Butter Cups, Marlboro and Lucky Strike cigarettes, Colgate toothpaste, Pert shampoo, Kahlua Liquer, Miss Clairol hair color. Chris Dodd of the Motion Pictures Association of America would be disappointed to know that US DVDs make their way to Cuba and are pirated. The locals who rent DVDs burn five movies to one disc and rent them for five days for one CUC.

On any given day the Cubana and Aero Mexico flights from Mexico City and from Cancun to Havana are filled with elite Cubans who have been to Mexico on shopping trips. Their purchases far outweigh and outnumber their luggage and personal effects. They purchase food products at Sam's Club; they also purchase electronics, bicycles, auto parts, tires, home appliances, small hot water heaters, toilet paper, clothing, jewelry and much more. All Cubans deserve to see the Embargo end and be able to purchase US-produced goods for themselves where they live.

Apparently the Cuban government found a hole in the Embargo because they apparently acquired a substantial number of American made Smith & Wesson firearms in the past decade.

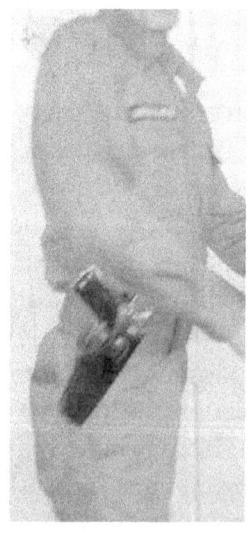

Cuban military sidearm – Made in the USA Embargo? What embargo?

14. Products Introduced to the Cuban People (Since 2011 on Mission Trips)

This is a list of items that have been brought on Mission trips to share with the Cuban people. None of these items are available in Cuba:

-SPAM™	-	Canned chicken
-Peanut butter	-	Tampons™
-Hand crank can openers	-	Scented candles
-Non-stick cookware	-	Hand sanitizer
-White-out™	-	Post-it Notes™
-Dremel Tool™	-	Scented markers
-Scrabble board game	-	Malt Milk Balls
-Sorry board game	-	Jello Pudding™
-Dinty Moore Beef Stew™	-	Applesauce
-Grape jelly	-	English muffins
-Glue gun	-	Lint rollers
-Cloth grocery bags	-	Aluminum foil
-Zip-Lock Bags™	-	Air deodorizer
-Scotch-Brite Sponges™	-	Sleep masks
-Duct tape	-	Starburst
-M & Ms	-	Swim noodles
-Microwave popcorn	-	Gatorade™
-Reese's Pieces	-	Bubble Soap

-Flannel Sheets   -Flannel Pajamas
-Strawberry Shortcake with Frozen Strawberries
-Coors Light™ Aluminum Bottle

The items most frequently asked for on a return trip are Tampons™ and peanut butter.

Section II.
Terrorism and
Espionage

15. Cubana Airlines Flight 455

Before there was TWA 847 in which Muslim extremists killed US Navy Diver Robbie Stethem and tossed his body out the door of the airplane in 1985. Before there was Pan Am 103 blown up over Lockerbie, Scotland, resulting in the death of 270 from onboard the aircraft as well as on the ground. Before that sun-filled Tuesday morning in September 2001 when commercial airliners were hijacked and turned into jet fuel missiles, striking targets resulting in the death of 2,976 Americans.

Before the numerous fatal hijackings around the world since Oct. 6, 1976 there was Cubana Airlines Flight 455, blown out of the sky by a bomb as it climbed out of Barbados killing all 73 passengers and 5 crew members onboard.[22] The youngest victim was a seven year old girl.

The passenger manifest included all 24 members of Cuba's Gold Medal Fencing Team and 11 Guyanese medical students returning to classes in Havana. The average age of those on-board was 30 years. It's been well-documented that the brains behind this act of airborne terrorism were two virulent anti-Castro Cuban exiles, Orlando Bosch and Luis Posada Carilles, as detailed in the

---

22   *wikipedia.org/wiki/Cubana_Flight_455*

national Security Archive.[23] These men could be considered the Abu Nidal and Sheik Khalid Mohammed of the Caribbean.

Both had been trained by the US Military and the CIA in the art of making bombs. Defending himself, Bosch would later say, infamously "All of Castro's planes are warplanes." He also said, "There were no innocents on that plane."

This act of air terrorism was at the time the deadliest terrorist airline attack in the Western Hemisphere. Unfortunately for the victims of this terrorist act and their families justice has never been served.

Bosch and Posada along with Freddy Lugo and Hernan Ricardo the two men who actually planted the bombs onboard the flight were arrested. When the plane exploded Lugo sent a cable to Bosch and Posada saying, '73 dogs just went off a cliff.' In a trial held in Venezuela, Lugo and Ricardo were sentenced to 20 years in prison. Bosch got off on a technicality and fled to Miami where has was hailed as a hero. Posada was held for eight years but then allegedly bribed his way out of jail and spent the next 14 years in alleged terrorist activities in Latin America.

Regrettably the families of the victims of the Flight 455 bombing have received neither justice for their loved ones or closure for themselves. Orlando Bosch died in Miami on April 26, 2011 and Luis Posada lives in Miami having been protected by his terrorist collaborator US Representative Ileana Ros-Lehtinen. But Flight 455 was not the lone act of terrorism perpetrated by Bosch and Posada.

In the air and on the ground, just like Abu Nidal and Sheik Khalid Mohammed, Bosch and Posada were equal opportunity assassins. And Posada was as creative in the construction of bombs as has been Al Qaeda's chief bomb-maker Ibrahim Hassan al Asiri.

---

23   gwu.edu/~nsarchiv/NSAEBB/NSAEBB153/

16. Bosch and Posada – Ministers of Terror

One chapter can barely scratch the surface of the history of terroristic acts allegedly perpetrated against innocent Cubans and citizens of other countries under the guise of the War on Castro orchestrated by these two cold-blooded killers. Among them are:

- Bosch was arrested by Miami police in 1964 for allegedly towing a homemade torpedo through downtown during rush hour
- In 1966 police found six 100-pound aerial practice bombs in the trunk of Bosch's Cadillac which had been stopped at a roadblock
- Bosch fired a bazooka in the Port of Miami on a Polish freighter that was headed to Havana on Sept. 16, 1968
- Posada was implicated in the assassination of the Chilean Foreign Minister in Washington, D.C., on Sept. 21, 1976
- Bosch and Posada were implicated in the bombing of Cubana Flight 455 on Oct. 6, 1976
- Bosch was linked by Miami law enforcement to a bombing of Mackey Airlines offices after the announced resumption of flights to Cuba in 1977

- Posada was involved with guerilla terrorists in Central America in the scandal that came to be known as Iran-Contra in the 1980s
- Bosch and Posada have histories of involvement with the CIA in the 1960s and 1970s
- Bosch and Posada were both trained by the US Army at Fort Benning, Ga., in the 1960s
- Posada admitted involvement in a series of bombings at various tourist hotels and restaurants in Havana in which Italian tourist Fabio di Celmo was killed in 1997
- Posada was discovered with 200 pounds of explosives in Panama City, Panama which he intended to detonate in a university auditorium filled with students during a speech by Fidel Castro in November 2000
- In 2006 FBI agents went to Cuba to investigate Posada's role in the 1997 tourist bombings. FBI documents reveal that Posada was quite adept at fabricating and concealing bombs in shoes, shampoo bottles, and clothing. Shoe bombs, bottles bombs, and underwear bombs; where have we heard of those?

Bosch resume[24]

Posada Resume[25]

The above is just a cross section of the terrorist resumes Bosch and Posada Carilles allegedly developed in countries that did business with Cuba, as well as airline offices and embassies in the US.

Rather than dwell on these crimes – which the US government has all but ignored – let us instead examine the manner in which the two Bush Administrations at the behest of U.S. Representative Ileana Ros-Lehtinen and the Miami Cartel have coddled and protected these terrorists.

After being released from prison for the freighter attack Bosch fled the U.S. and made his way around Latin America. When he returned in 1989 he was charged with parole violations by federal law enforcement authorities. He was an undocumented alien

---

24   *spartacus.schoolnet.co.uk/JFKbosch.htm*
25   *spartacus.schoolnet.co.uk/JFKposada.htm*

in the U.S. and an international terrorist. Cuba sought his extradition to face charges for the Flight 455 bombing.

Enter the most prolific coddler of terrorists in the history of the United States Congress, Representative Ileana Ros-Lehtinen of Miami. This terrorist sympathizer pled Bosch's case with President George H.W. Bush through her Campaign Manager Jeb Bush, the president's son. President Bush pardoned Bosch on July 18, 1990.[26] The Bush pardon was granted to this terrorist over the objection of the Bush Justice Department who did not want the US to appear to be harboring a terrorist. Attorney General Dick Thornburgh opposed the pardon and labeled Bosch 'an unrepentant terrorist.'[27] On the bright side for the Bush family the voting bloc of Cuban-Floridians went solidly for President Bush in 1992. Unfortunately that was not enough for re-election as President Bush 41 lost to Bill Clinton. In a brazen display of amorality while Bosch was awaiting a determination by the Bush administration, terrorist collaborator Ros-Lehtinen celebrated the murder of dozens of innocent men, women, and children by sponsoring Orlando Bosch Day in Miami.

Posada was convicted and jailed in Panama for the attempt in 2000 to blow up a university auditorium filled with students where Fidel Castro was to speak. In 2003 Ros-Lehtinen and the two Diaz-Balarts wrote a letter to the president of Panama on Congressional Letterhead pleading for the release of their beloved terrorist Posada.[28] In 2004 Posada and three fellow terrorists involved in the plot were pardoned by outgoing President Mireya Moscoso. Ms. Moscoso denied to the press that any pressure had been exerted by either of the Bush brothers – George W. or Jeb – but stated, "I knew that if these men stayed here, they would be extradited to Cuba and Venezuela, and they were surely going to kill them there."

Posada snuck into the United States through Texas in 2005 and then requested political asylum. The US government in a

---

26   hnylatinojournal.com/home/politics/americas/the_bush_familys_favorite_terrorist.html

27   www.enotes.com/topic/Orlando_Bosch

28   27 mltoday.com/subject-areas/cuba/posada-hearing-on-capitol-hill-367.html

rare moment of righteousness arrested him and sought to deport him to Venezuela in response to an extradition request.

On Sept. 28, 2005 an immigration judge appointed by President George W. Bush ruled that Posada could not be deported to Venezuela because he could possibly be tortured there. To quote Dick Cheney, the vice president of the United States at the time, "So?" Cubans strongly feel that if anyone in the Western Hemisphere deserves enhanced interrogation it is Luis Posada Carilles. But Posada has come to be known in Cuba as the Bush Family's Favorite Terrorist and most Cubans believe that he like his partner Bosch will go to his grave without having been held accountable for the slaughter of their innocent countrymen.

The US Department of Homeland Security brought charges against Posada for entering the U.S. illegally. He bonded out of jail and was escorted to South Florida by federal agents where the murderous terrorist was greeted with a hero's welcome. He was placed under house arrest. Another Bush appointee, U.S. District Judge Kathleen Cardone, gutted the indictment and ordered Posada's electronic bracelet removed. Judge Cardone was overturned by the Fifth Circuit Court of Appeals.

In 2010 Posada went on trial in El Paso, Texas. The Miami Cartel rallied behind their cold-blooded murderer and raised thousands of dollars for his defense. His attorney threatened to have Posada reveal details of some of the crimes he committed with the CIA's assistance back in the 60s, 70s, and 80s. The kangaroo trial ended in acquittal.

In spite of the fact that the FBI labeled Posada 'the worst terrorist of this Hemisphere' the Bush administration's Assistant Secretary of State for Western Hemisphere Affairs Roger Noriega said when Posada was arrested that the charges against the terrorist 'may be a completely manufactured issue.' The extent to which the Bush administration went to cover for and protect these terrorists is astonishing.

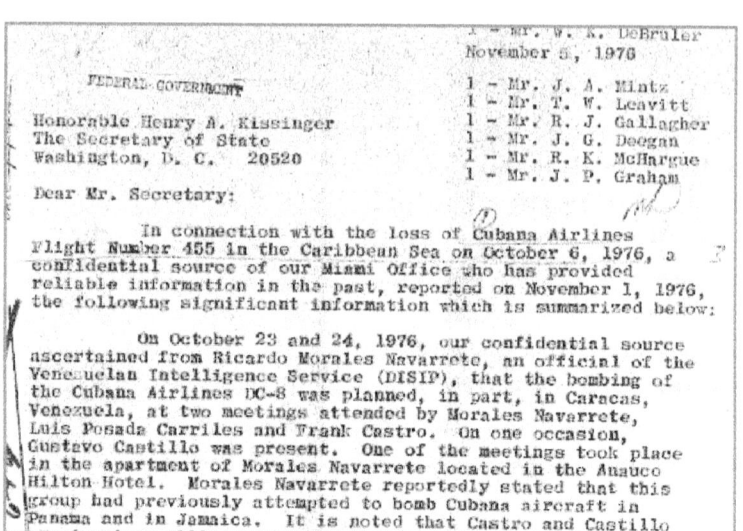

Memo to Secretary of State Henry Kissinger naming Luis Posada as one of the masterminds of the Cubana Flight 455 Bombing

Orlando Bosch and Luis Posada, International Terrorists, protected from prosecution by the Diaz-Balart/Ros-Lehtinen Axis of Terror and Vengeance in Congress

17. Jorge Mas Canosa

In Miami there is a section of Biscayne Parkway named Jorge Mas Canosa Blvd. There also is a middle school named after Mas Canosa, probably the only public school in America named after a financier of terrorism. Jorge Mas Canosa has been packaged by the Cuban-Floridian community what Reverend Martin Luther King, Jr. was to blacks.

Dr. King fought prejudice and bigotry. Mas Canosa fought the Castro regime in Cuba. King's approach was non-violent. Mas Canosa's approach at times has been very violent. Dr. King set in place a movement which achieved great things. Mas Canosa was involved in a movement that has gone nowhere and achieved nothing in 54 years, save for the killing of innocent civilians in Cuba and elsewhere which he allegedly financed, and the shakedown of millions of US taxpayer dollars.

Mas Canosa was born in Santiago, Cuba, in 1939. His family fled to the United States after the Castro Revolution. In 1961 he volunteered to fight in the disastrous Bay of Pigs Invasion.

National Archive documents from CIA files state that 'in July 1965, terrorist Luis Posada reported that he had constructed two 10-pound Limpet bombs. These were for a Mas Canosa operation against Soviet and Cuban ships in the port of Veracruz,

Mexico, using eight pounds of Pentolite explosives and a pencil detonator.[29]

Mas Canosa helped found the Cuban American National Foundation. Although the tax-exempt foundation has declared that it seeks to bring down Cuba's Communist government solely through peaceful means, Luis Posada has said leaders of the foundation discreetly financed his terror operations.[30] Mas personally supervised the flow of money and logistical support, Posada said.

"Jorge controlled everything," Posada told the *New York Times*.[31] ``Whenever I needed money, he said to give me $5,000, give me $10,000, give me $15,000, and they sent it to me.''

Over the years, Posada estimated, Mas sent him more than $200,000 to finance mayhem and murder. ``He never said, 'this is from the foundation,' Posada recalled. Rather, he said with a chuckle, the money arrived with the message, 'this is for the church.'' Jorge Mas Canosa might be considered the Caribbean counterpart of Osama Bin Laden – financing terrorism but keeping his hands clean.

In the early 1990s, Mas Canosa did a TV interview with Tom Brokaw in which he stated that he was prepared, when Fidel Castro died, to fly into Cuba with 'his people' and set up a new government. It's difficult to imagine that ordinary impoverished Cubans would have warmed up to a high rolling millionaire in a thousand dollar suit with gold cufflinks along with his entourage.

What arrogance and self-aggrandizement! The Solidarity trade union rose to power in Poland in 1989. It eventually negotiated with the Communist government and won open elections and formed a coalition government. It did not go to Chicago, home of the second-largest Polish population in the world to find a president. Members elected one of their own, Lech Walesa, who had founded the organization. Most new governments founded by free peoples around the world have selected their new leaders from within their ranks. Should this situation ever come to pass

---

29   *gwu.edu/~nsarchiv/NSAEBB/NSAEBB153/*
30   *en.wikipedia.org/wiki/Luis_Posada_Carriles*
31   *www.nytimes.com/1998/07/13/world/bomber-s-tale*

in Cuba the same will happen. No Mas Canosa or Diaz-Balart or Ros offspring will swoop in and be greeted as a hero. Quite the contrary, they would likely be lynched.

Jorge Mas Canosa died in 1997. Since his death his family established the Jorge Mas Canosa Freedom Foundation. A review of the Foundation's IRS 990's shows transfer of funds back and forth with the CANF. A forensic accountant would probably be needed to sort the money trail.

In 2006 Fidel Castro ceded power to his brother Raul. Fidel Castro was last seen publicly in February 2013 on national TV. Mas Canosa has been outlived by Fidel Castro by 15 years and counting! Living well (and long) is the best revenge.

18. Brothers to the Rescue

It began with the noblest of intentions. Cuban refugees were fleeing their country on rickety homemade rafts and many were dying in the passage between Cuba and the area of the United States known as the Florida Straits.

A Cuban exile in Miami named Jose Basulto teamed up with a group of fellow pilots and formed a group called Hermanos al Rescate – Brothers to the Rescue (BTTR) in 1991.[32] They claimed they were a humanitarian group and began flying reconnaissance flights looking for floating refugees between Cuba and the US. When they spotted 'floaters' they would direct the US Coast Guard to pick the rafters up.

The group received wide financial support in Miami but the group's donations declined from $1.5 Million in 1994 to $350,000 in 1995 when the U.S. government changed its immigrant policy to *wet foot/dry foot*. This meant that rafters who were picked up in the water (wet feet) would be returned to Cuba.

If the BTTR carried out their mission they would be condemning rafters to being repatriated. So the group instead redirected its focus to harassing the Cuban government and terrorizing the Cuban people. They began flying along and into Cuban airspace, taunting Cuban air traffic controllers. On at least one occasion

---

32   .fiu.edu/~fcf/brothers.html

Jose Basulto and a passenger in his plane dropped 500,000 leaf-lets on Havana. One of the group's pilots was Juan Pablo Roque, a former Cuban MiG pilot. Roque disappeared from Florida on Feb. 23, 1996 and turned up in Cuba. He criticized the BTTR group and talked of their plans to carry out paramilitary attacks on Cuba.

The next day brought the darkest day in US-Cuba hostilities since the Missile Crisis. Two Cessna Skymaster aircraft formerly used by the US military were shot down by a Cuban MiG. The MiG had been scrambled along with another to intercept the air-craft. A third aircraft piloted by Basulto managed to get away – convenient for him. The Cuban government had passed warn-ings to the U.S. government repeatedly about these planes enter-ing Cuban airspace. An FAA official later testified in court that he had warned Basulto of the possibility of being shot down while violating Cuban airspace.

Transcripts show that as the three American aircraft approached Cuban airspace Basulto was warned of encroaching Cuban airspace.

Havana Center: "I inform you that the zone north of Havana is active. You run danger by penetrating that side of north parallel 24."

Basulto:" We are aware of the danger each time we cross the area south of 24 but we are willing to do it. It is our right as free Cubans."

Havana Center:" Then, we copy information, sir."

Basulto was flipping the middle finger at the Cuban authori-ties. Shortly thereafter the two MiGs were dispatched and two of the planes were shot down. Basulto had high-tailed it in coward-ice. He left his compatriots in danger. Passengers aboard Royal Caribbean Cruise Lines Majesty of the Seas saw one plane's descent and smoke trail and shot video which was later shown on CNN.

Condemnation of the actions of the Cuban military was swift and loud especially from the Miami Cartel and among right wing politicians in the United States. This led to passage of the Helms-Burton Act which tightened sanctions on Cuba and extended sanctions to foreign companies or countries doing business with Cuba. The Congressional crazies in the Miami Cartel called it an Act of War against the United States and demanded that President Clinton order the bombing or invasion of Cuba by the US Military. Fortunately President Clinton was in command of greater sanity than the Miami Cartel.

A great deal of attention was focused on the dialogue between the Cuban MiG pilots who celebrated the shoot down of pilots who had annoyed and antagonized their country for years and who had talked of attacking the country from the air. The MiG pilots joked about having cajones and 'blowing his balls off' and that 'he would no longer be a pain in their necks' referring to one of the US pilots.

Secretary of State Madeline Albright condemned the attack saying 'this was not cajones it was cowardice.' Apparently the secretary has never heard tapes of U.S. military pilots celebrating a shoot down. The language is similar. This is not a condemnation of the BTTR operation nor is it a plaudit for the Cuban military. It is an overview of a tragic situation that got out of hand. Unfortunately the true facts were slow in coming because the Miami Cartel took control of the narrative just like they had in 1959, and spun the story to their advantage.

The public was deceived into believing that the flights were still rescuing rafters. The BTTR had not spotted a raft in the water since August 1995. Prior to 1995 when they entered Cuban airspace it was ostensibly to search for rafters; they were now just flying into Cuban airspace to antagonize the Cuban government.

On Jan. 9 and 13 of 1996, BTTR planes flew into Cuban airspace and dropped leaflets over Havana. The number reported in the January 13 drop was 500,000. Cubans who remember that day still recall it with fear. They say they ran inside buildings because they did not know what was falling. The fliers could have been tainted with some kind of biological agent.

Now let's assess this situation through the prism of the 9-11 attacks. After it became clear that radical terrorists had hijacked four commercial airliners the U.S. military was put on full alert. Air Force fighter pilots across the country were sent to patrol the skies until all commercial aviation was grounded. Prior to climbing into their aircraft they faced off eye-to-eye with their commanding officer. They were told that they might receive an order to shoot down a commercial airliner if it were under terrorist control. On-board could be friends, neighbors, family members, colleagues. Could they in fact pull the trigger? Every pilot who scrambled that day replied yes. They realized that defending their country might mean having to take the lives of innocent civilians, even Americans.

Since 9-11 the US military has scrambled jets many times to intercept private planes that wandered into restricted airspace. These have usually been piloted by American citizens who wandered off course. But were the military to intercept a plane flown by a foreign national who was hostile to the U.S. there is no doubt they would be blown from the sky.

In a similar vein exactly one week after the 9-11 attacks were perpetrated the anthrax attacks began in the U.S. Letters laced with anthrax were sent to media outlets and two US senators via mail delivery. The country was in a double panic – terrorist attacks from on high and toxin attacks through the mail. There has not been a serious anthrax incident since 2001, but if 500,000 fliers were to drop from the sky over a major US city would people stick around to see what was printed on them or would they take cover. More importantly would the US government let that airplane fly off on its way or would it take action against it? Regrettably for Mr. Basulto and especially his Brothers to the Rescue they poked the bear one time too many and the bear swatted back.

The response by the US Congress to the BTTR shoot down was way over the top. Certainly there are some who profit handsomely from the US Blockade on Cuba. Some benefit through grants from the federal government. Some, like the Fanjul Brothers (US sugar barons) and the Bacardi Family (Rum barons) profit handsomely from the laws and restrictions put in place by Congress against Cuban products. The Bacardi legal counsel drafted the Helms-Burton Act. And these people in spite of their heritage or what family they may have still living in Cuba could not care less about the 11 Million people of Cuba.

There are many in the US government who claim the Christian mantle. How could they have so easily gone along with an act of cruelty to 11 Million people through this legislation out of hatred for one man by the amoral Miami Cartel? The Helms-Burton and other restrictions need to be dismantled for the welfare of the 11 Million people of Cuba,

19. The Cuban Five

A s one travels across Cuba or walks the streets in its cities it is impossible to ignore the various tributes and testaments to the *Five Heroes*. The Five Heroes are more commonly known as the Cuban Five[33] and were part of a 14-member group known as *La Red Avispa* (Wasp Network) which was sent to the United States from Cuba to infiltrate and spy on Brothers to the Rescue, Jorge Mas Canosa and his Cuban American National Foundation, and other Miami-based terror organizations that continually plotted against innocent civilians in Cuba.

They also intended to infiltrate the re-election campaign of Congressman Lincoln Diaz-Balart, an inept hater of his uncle Fidel Castro who is the son of the Rafael Lincoln Diaz-Balart, former Deputy Interior Minister in the Batista Dictatorship who was the alleged overseer of torture, rape, and firing squads during his tenure. They had hoped to uncover skeletons in Lincoln Diaz-Balart's closet and neutralize his influence.

The FBI received information about the group's activities and began monitoring them in 1995. The men turned over to the FBI all the information they had collected on various Cuban-American terrorist groups in Miami. The FBI used the information against them. Four members of the Wasp Network fled to Cuba, five

---

33   *wikipedia.org/wiki/Cuban_Five*

cooperated with the FBI and plead guilty to being unregistered agents and received minimal prison time, and the final five were arrested in 1998 and eventually put on trial.

The five were charged variably with among other things being unregistered agents of a foreign government, conspiracy to defraud the United States, espionage, and first-degree murder as accomplices in the BTTR shoot downs. They were all convicted and received various sentences. The Five Heroes are Gerardo Hernández, Antonio Guerrero, Ramón Labañino, Fernando González and René González. They are revered in their homeland for having given up their freedom to protect their country from Miami-based terrorists.

The trial was of farcical proportions. US District Court Judge Joan Lenard among many indiscretions refused to move the trial away from South Florida. This was just months after the Elian Gonzalez saga had played out down there.

CNN reported at the time, the danger was that, "The pervasive and violent anti-Castro struggle of the Miami community would not only infect the jury with hostility but would cause jurors to fear for their [and their families] safety, livelihoods, and community standing if [they're] acquitted." The trial lasted seven months but the jury only deliberated a few hours, returning guilty verdicts on all 25 counts.

While the jury was deliberating, Justice Department lawyers sought to drop the murder charge against Gerardo Hernández because the incident occurred outside of US jurisdiction but Judge Lenard refused.

The Circuit Court of Appeals agreed with the defense that the trial had taken place in a hostile environment and overturned the convictions. However the full Circuit Court reinstated the convictions.

In August 2001 when the Bush Administration should have been heeding the warnings of Condoleezza Rice regarding Al Qaeda they were obsessing over these five men, likely at the behest of Ileana Ros-Lehtinen. Upon their final conviction the five were ordered held separately in solitary confinement awaiting sentencing. They could receive no correspondence from their families or their lawyers.

In March 2003 the men who had been held in solitary confinement awaiting trial and then sentencing were ordered by the Bush Justice Department to serve their sentences in four different federal prisons across the United States, in solitary confinement. Their families have been denied visas to come visit them.

One of the five, Rene Gonzalez, was released from federal prison in Miami on Oct. 7, 2011, and was given three years' probation. Judge Lenard refused to allow him to go home to serve out his probation in Cuba; instead she ordered him to live in the Miami area for the term of his probation so she could monitor him and ensure *that he is no longer a threat to society*. So Rene will live for a little more than 1,000 days surrounded by virulent Cuban exiles, most who care little about their countrymen at home but have a passionate hatred for anyone associated with the Castro Regime.

Yet Rene last year showed Judge Lenard, Ros-Lehtinen, and all the terrorist sympathizers in Miami what an honorable man he is. His brother is terminally ill in Cuba. He filed a request with the court to travel home to Cuba for 14 days to see his brother in his last days. Over the vociferous objections of the Miami Cartel - people who had no right to have any say in the matter, Judge Lenard approved Rene's request. Rene traveled to Cuba to visit with his brother in mid-March and returned exactly two weeks later.

Terrorist sympathizer Ileana Ros-Lehtinen, in opposing the request stated: "Allowing Rene Gonzalez to travel to Cuba would be a dangerous mistake and would jeopardize US national security." One can speculate how many times US national security has been jeopardized by Ms. Ros-Lehtinen's terrorist soul mates engaging in criminal activity. For that matter, how many of Ms. Ros-Lehtinen's terrorist soul mates or any Americans, being given a two-week leave from prison in a foreign country would have lived up to their agreement and returned after their leave ended?

Rene was allowed to return to Cuba again in early May 2013. He'd held dual citizenship and in exchange for disavowing his American citizenship at the US Interests Section, he was allowed to remain in Cuba.

The Five Heroes are on billboards and buildings all over Cuba. Schoolchildren hear about them every day

20. The Case of Alan Gross

In a reverse setting and on a smaller scale, the case of Alan Gross closely resembles the case of the Cuban Five. Although for Gross, save the synagogue that he attends in Maryland, there probably are not many posters or billboards reminding people of his plight.

Alan Gross[34] is a 63-year-old social worker and international development professional. He was a contractor for the US Agency for International Development (USAID) working on a project to deliver computers and communication equipment to members of the Jewish community in Cuba.

Computers brought into Cuba have to be declared, and bringing satellite phones into the country is illegal, as well for two-way radios or walkie-talkies. Gross traveled to Cuba four times transporting telephone parts. He also enlisted the aid of American Jews traveling on mission trips to carry telephone components for him and instructed them how to disassemble and conceal them in their hand carried luggage. They were identified because every bag whether checked or hand-carried is X-rayed at Josc Marti Airport upon arrival. He reported to USAID that wireless networks had been set up in three communities with approximately 325 users.

---

34   wikipedia.org/wiki/Alan_Phillip_Gross

His fifth trip began in Cuba in November 2009 and on Dec. 3 he was arrested at the Havana Airport departing the country. When he was arrested he had in his possession a high-tech chip intended to keep satellite phone transmissions from being located within 250 miles. The chip is not available on the open market. It is provided most frequently to the CIA and the Defense Department, but also can be obtained by the State Department, overseers of USAID. Asked how Gross obtained the card a USAID spokesman denied the agency played any role in helping Gross acquire equipment.

An attorney named Armanda Nuria Piñero-Sierra visited Gross in jail and was hired as his lawyer. She handled his trial and appeals. Piñero-Sierra also represents the families of the Cuban Five which led to speculation that the Cuban government might have been setting up a prisoner exchange.

Gross was charged in February 2011, with 'Acts against the Independence and Territorial Integrity of the State' ('Actos Contra la Independencia o la Integridad Territorial del Estado'), and faced up to 20 years in prison. His trial began on March 4, 2011 with his wife, her attorney and three US observers present. On March 12, 2011 he was sentenced by the Cuban court to 15 years in prison.

Numerous US officials have sought Gross' release including President Jimmy Carter, Governor Bill Richardson, Senators Dick Durbin, Patrick Leahy and Richard Shelby, and Representatives Chris Coons and Barbara Lee. Regrettably each outreach to Cuban officials was unilateral, 'we want to take home our citizen who was convicted of spying, but we will not even talk about your five citizens who were convicted of equally dubious charges in our kangaroo court of South Florida. We are the United States, give us what we want. How dare you expect something in return for giving us our guy?'

In October 2011, it was revealed that the US State Department had offered to allow one of the five, Rene Hernández, who is serving probation in Miami to serve the remainder of his probation in Cuba, in exchange for Gross' release. The offer was rejected by Cuban authorities. Why not swap the five prisoners held by the US for Alan Gross? Is it pressure from the Miami Cartel that is impeding any such consideration? The all-important Florida votes in national election? Prisoner exchanges are rarely equal on both sides of the scale. Read more on this topic in Chapter 22.

Gross has had the opportunity to see his wife and representatives of the American Jewish community while he has been in prison, as well as placing a weekly telephone call to his wife or to American media. Gross has received more humane treatment at the hands of the Cubans than the Cuban Five have in US hands. He has lost more than 100 pounds while imprisoned but that may be a result of the Cuban diet of rice and beans. He is not being held at a Cuban prison. He is being detained at a hospital in a military base. That may in fact be to stave off any attempt at a Navy Seals-type extraction. His family hopes to have him home as his elderly mother is dying and his daughter is battling cancer. Perhaps sanity will break out in Washington before other Americans end up in Cuban jails to level the playing field with the Cuban Five.

Alan Gross and his wife Judy in a picture that predates his arrest in Cuba. Even the Cuba people want him freed to go home to his family, but get irate when US politicians go to Cuba, ask for his release, and refuse to discuss the Cuban Five

21. 'Spying' in the 21ˢᵗ Century

Anyone old enough to remember the Cuban Missile Crisis recalls that historic day – Oct. 25, 1962 at the United Nations. US Ambassador Adlai Stevenson dressed down and humiliated Soviet Ambassador Valerian Zorin.[35] Stevenson challenged Zorin on his and Soviet Foreign Minister Andrei Gromyko's denials that the Soviets were setting up offensive missile launch sites in Cuba. The highlight came when Stevenson's staffers placed aerial spy photos taken by a U-2 plane on easels for the entire world to see. The missile sites were a bit difficult to identify, however they were outlined and labeled. Other members of the U.N. Security Council viewed the pictures using magnifying glasses. The jig was up for the Soviets as the world fell in place behind the United States. The Cuban Missile Crisis was about to come to an end.

Since that time the Cuban government has been wary of the United States and its ability to spy on their country. For years it refused to allow US commercial aircraft heading into the Caribbean to fly over the island, forcing them to take detours that cost fuel and time.

---

35   wikisource.org/wiki/Cuban_Missile_Crisis_speech_to_the_United_Nations_Security_Council

The Cubans can relax and not worry about someone sneaking in spy equipment or flying over to view their landscape from above. With Google Earth™ and other technologies, even a 10-year-old child can look over any country, city, or neighborhood anywhere in the world! As this was being written a view of the Hotel Nacional in Havana was captured via Google Earth.™ There were one yellow and two white taxis parked in the exit side of the circular driveway. This was plainly visible on a laptop computer with no magnifying glass required.

During mission trips to Cuba some of the locals have been shown overhead views from Google Earth™ showing their neighborhoods, churches, and points of interest in their country. This has fascinated them. Unfortunately due to government restrictions Cubans do not have access to Google Earth™ through their limited Internet access. Nor do they have access to Skype,™ another wonderful tool that would help them better communicate with family outside Cuba.

22. Prisoner Exchanges

C hapter 19 discussed the circumstances of the Cuban Five, victims of an overzealous prosecution, an apparently intimidated jury, and a rabidly bloodthirsty Miami Cartel. The Five have been held in separate prisons in the United States with no access to their families or to one another. Amid all the muck that was spewed about in assailing these five individuals one thing is clear: not one life was lost as a result of any of their actions, notwithstanding the blather coming from the Miami Cartel political hacks.

Chapter 20 recaps the circumstances surrounding USAID contractor Alan Gross who is serving 15 years in a Cuban prison after being convicted of crimes against the state. Gross lost 100 pounds in his two years in prison and has family health matters back in the U.S. He wishes to be granted the same privilege as Rene Hernández of the Cuban Five. Cuban authorities have responded that Gross 'is not where Hernández was' apparently referring to Gross' continuing incarceration vis-à-vis Hernández having been released on probation.

It is now time for US leaders in Washington to act like responsible grown-ups, like Christians, free themselves from the shackles of the Miami Cartel, and do the right thing! For 20 years, the Ros-Lehtinen/Diaz-Balart Axis of Terror and Vengeance has driven the hateful anti-Christian agenda regarding Cuba. Is it not time that the Cuba policy be US-centric rather than Miami Cartel centric? Consider these numbers in a 1962 return of prisoners in exchange for non-human assets between the US and Cuba.

- 1,113 prisoners held by Cuba repatriated to the US
- $53 Million (1962 dollars) food and medicine sent to Cuba
- $47,619 per prisoner (1962 dollars)
- $1.00 in 1962 = $7.45 in 2012 dollars
- $394.9 Million (2012 dollars)
- $354,761 per prisoner (2012 dollars)

Those numbers are from Dec. 21, 1962, eight weeks after the Cuban Missile Crisis and 20 months after the Bay of Pigs Invasion. This is when Fidel Castro returned 1,113 Bay of Pigs prisoners back to the United States in exchange for $53 Million in food and medicine.[36] The Kennedy Administration had offered cash but Castro realized that with the Blockade in place food and medicine were more valuable. The entire $53 Million in food and medicine was donated by US companies in an era where patriotism and support for one's country meant more than just wearing flag pins on lapels.

The United States currently holds a 4.5:1 advantage over Cuba. Four incarcerated individuals and one on probation versus one incarcerated individual in a Cuban jail. All are non-violent offenders; not one drop of bloodshed has been caused by any of them or any national secrets stolen. All are political prisoners in one form or another.

To level the playing field the U.S. could broaden its requests from Cuba, such as releasing family members of Las Damas de Blanco (Chapter 24) from jails, or other concessions.

Those who say it is ridiculous to swap prisoners on an unequal footing might look to Israel. In 59 years Israel has had more than its share of wars, conflicts, and terror incidents. In those 59 years Israel has participated in prisoner exchanges with all its hostile neighbors.

---

36   wikipedia.org/wiki/Bay_of_Pigs_Invasion

Date	Return	Remains	Gained	Remains	Countries
Dec. 8, 1954	40		4	1	Syria
1956 Suez	5,577		4		Egypt
Feb. 21, 1962	1			1	Syria
Dec. 21, 1953	18		1		Syria
1967	6,728		17	2	Multiple
April 2, 1968	12			1	Jordan
Dec. 7, 1969	71		4		Multiple
Jan. 1, 1970	1		1		Fatah
June 9, 1972	5		3		Syria
June 3, 1973	46		3		Syria
Yom Kippur War	8,770		293		Egypt
April 4, 1975	92			39	Egypt
June 1975	20			2	Egypt
March 4, 1979	76		1		Palestine
Nov. 22, 1983	4,765		6		Palestine
May 21, 1985	1,150		2		Palestine
Sept. 12, 1991	2			1	Palestine
July 17, 1986		123	62	2	Hezb.
May 25, 1998	65	40		1	Hezb.

2003	2				Hezb.
2004	430	59		4	Hezb.
Oct. 2007	1	2		1	Hezb.
June 1, 2008	1			20	Hezb.
July 2008	5	199		2	Hezb.
Oct. 18, 2011	1,027			1	Palestine
Totals	28,905	423	401	78[37]	

Overall Tally

Israel returned: 28,905 prisoners and the remains of 423 Israel recovered: 401 prisoners and the remains of 58, a ratio of 64:1.

If the Israelis – with their high national pride and strong distaste for their Arab neighbors can exchange prisoners at the ratio of 64 to 1, certainly the United States can affect a 5 to 1 exchange and establish a baseline for a new era of relations with Cuba.

In 2008 Raul Castro mentioned in a conversation with Vatican Secretary of State Cardinal Tarcisio Bertone that he hoped for an eventual exchange with the United States for the Five Heroes. At the time Cuba held no US citizens in its prisons. But that changed on Dec. 3, 2009 with the arrest of Alan Gross.[38]

Time will tell whether the Obama administration does the right and humanitarian thing for all concerned, ignore the noise from the Congressional terrorists in the Miami Cartel and swap the prisoners. Or will Cuba seek to balance the scales by incarcerating additional Americans? It would be a historic and proper thing to do, exchange Alan Gross for the Cuban Five which would likely be supported by the American people if they were given the facts.

---

37   wikipedia.org/wiki/List_of_Israeli_prisoner_exchanges
38   catholicnewsagency.com/news/castro_interested_in_prisoner
_exchange_with_us_says_cardinal_bertone/

23. The Elian Gonzalez Saga

I f most Americans were unfamiliar with the Miami Cartel in South Florida the Elian Gonzalez saga certainly opened their eyes.[39] On Nov. 21, 1999, Elian along with his mother Elizabeth, her boyfriend and 11 others left Cuba at 4 a.m. hoping to get to the United States in a small aluminum boat with a faulty outboard motor.

Somewhere along the way and likely close to the U.S. shore the motor died and the boat began to take on water in a storm. People on the boat used nylon duffel bags to try and bail water. His mother and her boyfriend put Elian in an inner tube so that he would not drown. The boat swamped and Elizabeth and her boyfriend drowned along with nine others. Two adults and Elian were eventually rescued.

Elian told authorities and his father's extended family members in Miami that dolphins had saved him; that every time he began to slip from the inner tube the dolphins would push him back up. Elian's father Miguel had contacted his uncle Lazaro in Miami to tell him of the surprise departure and to watch for Elizabeth and Elian.

The Immigration and Naturalization Service gave temporary custody of Elian to Lazaro until he could be returned to his father. Miami Cartel leaders encouraged Lazaro to keep the boy and

39   en.wikipedia.org/wiki/Eli%C3%A1n_Gonz%C3%A1lez_affair

not return him to his father. The Miami Cartel ramped up into overdrive. Lazaro's daughter, a 21-year-old hairdresser named Marisleysis, became the focal point of media attention. Media reports later stated that they were often duped by Marisleysis with supposed hot information as she would run out the front door of her house shouting, "We have to go live," just in time for prime time newscasts.

Throughout all this Elian's father Juan Miguel – backed by the Cuban government – demanded that his son be returned home. The matter went into the Florida state and federal courts since the Miami relatives had filed a petition for asylum on Elian's behalf. The matter made its way to the 11th Circuit Court of Appeals in Atlanta.

No less a legal expert than Rush Limbaugh was ranting on his radio show that the 'Clintonistas' and especially Attorney General Janet Reno were denying Elian his constitutional rights by not allowing him to testify before the appeals court. This bloviating was notwithstanding the fact that only lawyers appear for oral arguments before the appeals court; witness testimony is never proffered. Even when testimony is allowed in domestic proceedings, children, especially those as young as 6 would never be allowed to testify.

The Miami Cartel Republican circus was in full swing. Senator Mel Martinez took the boy to Disney World seeking to bribe him into abandoning his father and remain in Florida. Miami-Dade County Mayor Alex Penelas, backed up by 22 civic leaders, gave a speech in downtown Miami vowing not to provide police assistance to federal authorities in any way to help remove Elian from the custody of the kidnappers and reunite Elian with his father. On April 14, 2000 the Miami relatives released a video in which Elian tells his father Juan Miguel that he does not want to return to Cuba and that he wants to stay in Miami. The makers of the video showed their ineptitude by not dubbing out the sound of a man off camera coaching Elian on what to say.

Reno tired of the games the Miami relatives were playing in negotiations. On April 20 she made the decision that Elian was to be removed from the home and instructed the INS to determine the best time to obtain the child. Upon being informed of this Marisleysis the hairdresser told a Justice Department community relations officer, "You think we just have cameras in the house? If people try to come in they could be hurt."

Agents went in during the early morning hours of April 22. As they searched the house the family members gave Elian to one of the fishermen who had found him. He hid in a bedroom closet with the boy and true to their role as media whores the relatives invited an Associated Press photographer into the bedroom. When a federal agent carrying a rifle and heavily dressed in body armor to protect himself from the crazies located the child a photo was snapped that went around the world.

Upon being removed from the relatives' home in Miami, Elian was spirited away on a government plane to Andrews Air Force Base near Washington, D.C. There he was reunited with his father, stepmother, and half-brother. The father's attorney Greg Craig released a photo of Elian on his father's shoulders, smiling broadly. In the Banana Republic of South Florida rioting broke out and Mayor Penelas' law enforcement officials had to use tear gas to disperse rioters. The relatives vowed to press on with their legal fight.

Juan Miguel, honorable gentleman that he is, agreed to remain in the United States with Elian until all legal matters were settled. He offered that up in a meeting with Reno. On June 1, 2000 the 11th Circuit Court of Appeals ruled that Elian was too young to request asylum and that only his father could speak on his behalf, and that the relatives had no legal standing. On June 28, the US Supreme Court declined to review the decision and Elian and his family returned home to Cardenas, Cuba, on the same day, having waited the process out to the end.

Like Rene Hernandez of the Cuban Five, Juan Miguel Gonzalez showed the U.S. Justice System that he is an honorable man whose words mean exactly what he says. On the occasion of the 10th anniversary of his return home, Elian told a US reporter that he was grateful to the American people for returning him home. How ironic that when most Cubans are skeptical of the United States' intentions, a young boy who was made the center of a Miami Cartel freak show expresses appreciation to the United States. Both Juan Miguel and Elian have shown the world that Cubans are fine, respectable people.

24. Las Damas de Blanco

One of the most touching sights on a Sunday morning in Cuba is seeing the ladies of Las Damas de Blanco[40] attend Mass together at St. Rita's Church in the Miramar section of Havana. One of the most heart-wrenching is seeing them being harassed and/or arrested by Cuban secret police.

The group is made up of the wives and other female relatives of Cuban dissidents and has its origins in 2003. During the Black Spring of that year the government arrested, tried, and convicted 75 human rights activists, independent journalists, and independent librarians. They were sentenced to terms of up to 28 years for *acts against the independence or territorial integrity of the state*, as well as accepting money from foreign governments including the United States. They came to be known as the Group of 75.

One of those imprisoned was Hector Maseda Gutierrez. His wife was Laura Pollan, a literature teacher. She began appearing at Cuban prison facilities where her husband Hector might have been incarcerated. In short order she found herself among the wives and family members of others in the Group of 75, all trying to determine where their loved ones were imprisoned.

Laura Pollan took it upon herself to organize Las Damas de Blanco (Ladies in White) shortly after the Group of 75 was jailed.

40   *damasdeblanco.com*

On Sundays the women would meet and attend mass at St. Rita's Church. After mass they would have a silent procession from the church to a nearby park.

If the Cuban government had disdain for the Group of 75, the disdain for this group of ordinary family matriarchs was even deeper though more difficult to act upon. The Cuban government condemned the group for being *a subversive association of American-backed terrorists*. The government took a hands-off approach to dealing with the ladies, but government organized groups did not. On Palm Sunday 2005 the Federation of Cuban Women sent 150 women to counter protest the group. Mobs have harassed them at various times and hurled insults at them.

On many occasions 'ordinary Cuban citizens' (read plain-clothes secret police) have gotten into dust-ups with the women and have conveniently assisted the police to load them into buses. Many of them have been detained, often times on their way to Sunday mass. Numerous women were detained trying to get to Pope Benedict's Masses in March 2012.

In 2005 the group was a co-recipient of the Sakharov Prize for Freedom of Thought. The Cuban government barred the group's leaders from traveling to receive the award in France. In 2010 Cardinal Jaime Ortega intervened with the government on their behalf and since that time they have been allowed to protest outside his church.

The Ladies in White and Cuban activist Dr. Oscar Elias Biscet were nominated for the 2012 Nobel Peace Prize by Rep. Ros-Lehtinen and the usual Miami Cartel suspects in Congress, apparent window dressing in order to give an impression of support. Los Damas de Blanco have also been claimed as beneficiaries by some of the groups in Miami who get federal dollars for 'democracy building in Cuba.' After a weekly Mass shortly after Pope Benedict's visit to Cuba in March 2012 several of the women were engaged in conversation by a knowledgeable American who inquired as to the Miami Cartel claims of financial support. According to the women it was non-existent. At the mention of terrorist collaborator Ros-Lehtinen's name one of the women spit on the ground and said 'La Cochino' – The Pig. This is Ileana

Ros-Lehtinen's nickname on the street in Cuba. She is universally loathed.

It is a disgrace that the shadowy groups in the Miami Cartel who receive government money put their emphasis on self-preservation rather than helping deserving people like these Cuban ladies.

Los Damas de Blanco prepare for Sunday Mass at St. Rita's Church along Embassy Row in Havana. They generally number more than forty and none of them take Holy Communion because they feel they are incomplete as families. It is a very emotional scene.

25. Miami Cartel & Terror in the 21st Century

The streets of South Florida have been quiet since the 1990s. With two of the leading proponents of terrorism deceased and one appearing to lay low in Miami it seemed that the younger generation had no taste for killing, maiming, or damaging people and properties. The 1997 bombings in Havana which Luis Posada claimed were directed by Jorge Mas Canosa were targeted at hotels and restaurants catering to foreign tourists. The mindset was if you hurt the tourist trade you hurt Castro and the people of Cuba. Tourism to Cuba has long been a sticking point with the anti-Cuban element in Miami.

Pope Benedict's visit to Cuba in March 2012 annoyed many in the Miami Cartel, including Senator Rubio and the other terrorist sympathizers in Congress. They criticized the Pope and his itinerary and demanded that the Holy Father follow the agenda they proscribed. It likely set them off when the Holy Father criticized the 53-year-old US Blockade against Cuba. Probably most troubling for them was the fact many American pilgrims made the trip to see the Pope and attend his Mass.

Among the many Americans who traveled to Cuba was a group of 310 Cuban-Americans from the Miami area. Their trip had been coordinated by the Archdiocese of Miami which turned to Coral Gables-based Airline Brokers Co. as a licensed provider of Cuba Travel. Miami media gave much coverage to the exiles and children of exiles heading to Cuba. The spotlight also shined on Airline Brokers Co. owner Vivian Mannarud.

At 3:00 am on the morning of April 25, Ms. Mannarud received a report from her alarm company of a broken window at her office. While en-route she received another call advising her of a fire in the building. She arrived to find her business completely gutted. The fire was ruled arson; the business that serves Cuban-Americans was fire-bombed.[41]

Normally a situation like this would bring a flurry of visits by local politicians expressing their condolences and words of support. Did any of the Miami Cartel office holders in Dade County show up? Of course they did not. Did the US representative for Coral Gables, terrorist collaborator Ros-Lehtinen or the US senator of Cuban ancestry Marco Rubio show up or speak out from Washington? Of course they did not.

Did the mastermind of terrorism Luis Posada stop by to express his condolence? No, he may have mentored the bomber. And it is possible in the bowels of Hell the two dead aficionados of terror Orlando Bosch and Jorge Mas Canosa may have been high-fiving.

Human Rights Watch lists Miami as a city where open expression can be dangerous to one's life. It would appear that in Miami the Cartel has the upper hand. The media treads lightly. Groups demonstrating for a new approach to Cuba have been attacked publicly and there was no police intervention. The same with a group that was demonstrating for the expulsion from the US of the terrorist Posada who allegedly bombed Cubana flight 455.[42]

During a visit to Miami last year, it was apparent that there is some kind of government-in-exile or government-in-waiting. It is the remnants of the Batista Dictatorship and their offspring. People will talk about it discreetly in the shops along Calle Ocho but they are fearful of publicly criticizing anyone as they were during the Batista Dictatorship in Cuba.

---

41   huffingtonpost.com/2012/05/13/coral-gables- travel- agenc_n_1513442.html
42   miami.indymedia.org/news/2007/02/7522.php

It is high time that the United States Congress stood up to the Miami Cartel and began some type of reconciliation on behalf of the good and welfare of the 11 Million citizens of Cuba.

Appendix A contains a 'terrorism scorecard' of attacks by anti-Castro groups in the US from 1967 – 1975

Section III.
Cronies, Crooks, and Our Tax Dollars

26. Cuba in Miami – Most Favored Nation Status

In international economics and international politics, 'most favored nation' (MFN) is a status or level of treatment accorded by one state to another. Viewed as a city-state the city of Miami and its Dade County neighbors have been extended favored nation status by the United States as a result of the noise and clout that has emanated from the Miami Cartel. Cuban-Floridians have enjoyed benefits that no other immigrant group enjoys. Take the 1980 Mariel Boatlift for instance. Some 125,000 Cubans including all the inmates of prisons and asylums that Fidel Castro forced boat captains to take onboard received asylum in the city-state of Miami.

For years Cubans have arrived in Florida on various floating devices, from boats to homemade rafts to converted motor vehicles. Through the years US immigration policy has varied with respect to which Cubans and under what circumstances would be allowed to immigrate and be granted legal permanent status but the policies have generally been skewed toward easy citizenship.

In 1995 the United States implemented the wet foot/dry foot policy. This means that Cubans interdicted at sea (wet foot) would be returned by the US to Cuba or a willing third country. If the Cubans made it ashore (dry foot) however they would get a chance to remain in the United States and later would qualify for expedited 'legal permanent resident' status and eventually U.S. Citizenship.

By contrast a boatload or a raft loaded with Haitians, whether intercepted at sea or weighing anchor on a Florida beach would have its passengers detained by US Custom and Immigration Service. They would be sent to a detention center and eventually deported back to Haiti. Rather ironic since there was a time when Haiti was ruled by a much more brutal dictator than Fidel Castro has been accused of being – 'Papa Doc' Duvalier and later his son 'Baby Doc.'

With the wet foot/dry foot policy Cubans leaving for the United States have avoided being caught by utilizing a new strategy. They dodge the Coast Guard by avoiding U.S. territorial waters. Rather than head north 90 miles across the Straits of Florida in very unpredictable waters sailors now go west. They sail the relatively calm waters of the Gulf of Mexico west and travel 226 miles toward Cancun. They never run the chance of having an encounter with the US Coast Guard. When they make landfall they join the trail of Mexicans and Central-Americans headed to the US, though they generally have people waiting for them who have driven from Miami. Though they claim Spanish heritage, most Cubans are whiter than the average American. Just look at US Senators Marco Rubio and Ted Cruz. Born in Canada to a Cuban father and an Irish mother, Cruz has Cuban blood yet is pasty white. While 35% of Cubans are non-white, there are far fewer people of color among the immigrants in South Florida.

The Mexicans and Central Americans will pay 'mules' to sneak them across the border, a very dangerous proposition. Some will make it, some will be beaten, raped, or robbed and never get across. But the Cubans will travel the Express Lane. Their van will drive to the US border crossing where they will climb out and step across the border. They can claim that they arrived with 'dry feet' and be put on the fast track to citizenship.

The Mexicans and Central Americans will come to the US and be degraded, insulted, told to go home, be accused of being criminals, and called parasites and illegals. Their heritage will draw the ire of those who detest bilingualism. The Cubans will head to the monolingual world of Miami and be treated as heroes who fled Castro's Cuba. No need to learn English in Miami as the public schools are bilingual. No placards in business windows reading: No English No Service – This Is America; No problem with 'presione dos par el espanol' on telephones; no difficulty getting a green card and then a fast-track to citizenship. Their light skin color always will set them apart from other Hispanics.

Those who live in the Congressional District of terrorist collaborator Ileana Ros Lehtinen will even have the luxury of having a dual language Congressional website. What happened to 'this is America – learn English!'

On March 30, 2012 a boat carrying eight Cubans departed Pinar del Rio, Cuba in the early morning hours headed for the Yucatan Peninsula of Mexico. Their last act onshore before departure was a group Rosary and prayers. On April 19 they stopped off in Texas on their way to Miami and the guarantee of US citizenship.

27. Radio & TV Marti

There are many Black Holes in the United States budget, but probably none wider and deeper or more protected than the sacred cow of the Miami Cartel, Radio/TV Marti. Like all government projects Radio Marti started out with great ideals. President Ronald Reagan received a suggestion from Miami activist Jorge Mas Canosa that the US establish a radio channel similar to Radio Free Europe that would have the capability of broadcasting into Cuba.

The staunch anti-communist Reagan could not resist such an idealistic concept. In 1983 President Reagan approved the creation of what was supposed to be called Radio Cuba, modeled after Radio Free Europe and Radio Liberty with studios in Washington, D.C. The radio broadcasts went live on May 20, 1985 to coincide with Cuban Independence Day, the day in 1902 that Cuba became independent of the United States.[43] It came to be known as Radio Marti after the Cuban hero Jose Marti.

Much to the chagrin of radio broadcasters in the Southeast, when Radio Marti went live Cuba began to jam the broadcasts. The jamming did not only impact Radio Marti but regular US stations as well.

---

43   *martinoticias.com*

Originally under the auspices of the US Information Agency, Radio Marti is now under the auspices of the International Broadcasting Bureau. Since its inception Radio Marti has had little impact in Cuba for two reasons: 1. the signals have been continually jammed by the Cuban government; and 2. While the aim should have been to educate the few Cubans who could actually receive the broadcasts, the programming was nothing but reverse propaganda – vicious and hateful screeds directed at Fidel Castro and other Cuban officials. Cubans reportedly found it very offensive.

Fidel Castro has long been a hero to his people and the U.S. has been his scapegoat. Hearing radio broadcasts emanating from the US and attacking El Commandante did not sit well with the Cuban people. Tokyo Rose in World War II did a better job or spreading information than has this outfit.

Even today, the Cubans who use Radio Marti as their verbal vehicle of assault on Cuba share very little information about freedom, democracy, or any of the ideals which it claims to want to extoll to the Cuban people. It is nothing more than a local radio station in South Florida broadcasting news for the Miami Cartel and ranting about the Castro Regime. In March 2013 the top items on its website were:

- Venezuelans to oppose Capriles
- Voting in the Falkland Islands
- Confessions of a Cuban who practiced prostitution
- Yoani Sanchez travels to Mexico for SIP Conference
- Obama's electoral catastrophe
- U.S aggression in Syria

Today Radio Marti broadcasts from transmitters in Delano, Calif.; Greenville, N.C.; and Marathon, Fla., from studios in Miami. Cuba jams the signal but it can be heard in Canada and some parts of Central and South America.

As if the Radio Marti financial black hole was not deep enough, on March 27, 1990 the U.S. government began broadcasting TV Marti. TV Marti has been an even bigger flop. Recently the US began flying an airplane that transmits towards Cuba for two hours each day. Cubans know it's there but are disgusted by its content. Every few years Democrats in both houses of Congress have looked at these pigs and threatened to shut them down but they manage to stay afloat, supported by people like terrorist collaborator Ileana Ros-Lehtinen.

From their inception through 2007, U.S. taxpayers have poured $500 Million into these two Miami Cartel black holes. In 2013 with a staff of approximately 100 their budget is $15 Million.

The huge financial boondoggle has been perpetuated by the fathers of U.S. Representatives Diaz-Balart and Ros-Lehtinen who have at various times been on Radio TV Marti's payroll preaching their messages of hate and retaliations rather than educating Cubans on the principles of freedom.

In 2012 the way to gauge popularity was by looking at the number of Facebook friends or likes. On Facebook Radio TV Marti has a mere 130 likes – the same number of employees! Their opposite on the island of Cuba is just a website, Cubadebate. com and it has 89,981 likes. It may be Cuban propaganda, but the site is very well done and far more professional looking than Radio TV Marti. This vehicle for broadcasting propaganda to the Cuban people is managed by a man named Carlos Garcia-Perez. In an on-air editorial Garcia-Perez derided Cardinal Jaimie Ortega Alamino, leader of the Catholic Church in Cuba, and said the Cardinal has a 'lackey attitude.'[44] The GAO reported in 2007 that the broadcasts had been heard by barely 2% of the Cuban population.

A generous financial reward has been offered to anyone who can locate a Cuban national under the age of 50 who has heard a Radio Marti broadcast. It cannot be someone just off the raft or someone arriving by air with a visa who would say whatever one wanted them to say. It has to be a real Cuban national living in Cuba. Many people in many Catholic parishes in Cuba have heard this offer. As financially desperate as they are, no Cubans are even willing to lie about having heard it, if only for the money.

---

44   catholicculture.org/news/headlines/index.cfm?storyid=14224

28. Cuba-Centric NGOs

N GO is an acronym for Non-Government Organization. An NGO is a legally constituted organization created by natural or legal persons that operates independently of any government. While there are some 40,000 NGOs worldwide, in the United States some operate as non-profits with a 501(c)3 designation from the IRS.

The funding can be private, public, or a mix. If an NGO has a non-profit designation it is required to file a form IRS 990 annually. Non-profit 990s can be searched on Guidestar. com. Following is data extracted from non-profit NGOs in Florida and Washington, D.C., that claim to focus on Cuba. These are not complete returns, just a cross section of data to illustrate the waste that has permeated the whole anti-Castro 'cottage industry.' Some NGOs show government grants on their 990s others do not, they just lump all income together.

The challenge for US officials to evaluate how these programs are running and where the money is going – if at all – is the fact the two countries have reciprocal restrictions on the travels of diplomats in their respective interests section. Save for the occasional religious missionary who may have a conversation with some of the supposed beneficiaries of these funds there is no means for the US government to verify the transferring or receipt of the funds. The only verification comes through the agencies' self-reporting.

Center for a Free Cuba

	2007-2009
Total Income	$4,411,295
U.S. Government (incl. in total)	$3,596,277
Executive Comp.	$231,515
Accountant	$328,297
Supplies	$469,461
Postage/Ship	$190,867
Printing	$284,749
Travel	$340,456
Other	$708,310
Outreach (undefined)	$577,444

No money for Humanitarian Aid to Cuba in any year
$708,310 for Other, undefined
Source: Center for a Free Cuba IRS Form 990 for 2007, 2008, 2009
Additional entries of note:
From 2008 Report Statement F: *Statement of Activities outside the United States as follows:*

Region

Central America/Caribbean Region – Expenses of $129,583 to Strengthen Society

Europe -(Iceland/Greenland $329,643 for Cuban Democracy

There is no trace located of any relationship between Cuba and Iceland or Greenland via any Internet search.

In 2008 Felipe Sixto who had been the Center for a Free Cuba's Chief of Staff was uncovered to have defrauded the Center out of $574,274 from 2003 to 2007. He continued to run his scam after he left the Center and in his new job as Special Assistant to President George W. Bush. Chapter 29 will deal with Felipe Sixto's crimes.

Cuban Liberty Council

	2008-2010
Total Income	$554,552
US Government	$382,749
Fundraiser	$114,362
Executive Compensation	$148,617
Salaries	$190,149

No funds dedicated to Humanitarian Aid in any of the three years.

Source: Cuban Liberty Council IRS Form 990 for 2008, 2009, 2010

Directorio Democratico Cubano Inc.

	2008-2010
Total Income	$6,776,507
US Government	$6,198,878
(included in total)	
Executive Comp.	$426,296
Salaries	$1,227,758
Rent	$364,637
Travel	$490,792
Other	$1,191,694
Equipment	$543,939
Auto Loan	$41,225
Radio Programs	$152,391
Television Ads	$75,659
Wire cash transfers:	
North America	$3,125
Central America	$228,141
South America	$208,760
Europe	$25,410
Humanitarian Aid	$43,592
To Cuba	

Percentage of income paid in salaries 33%

Percentage of income paid to organizations in Central & South America, and Europe is 6.8% - no identification of recipients.

Percentage of income dedicated to Humanitarian Aid to Cuba .06%

$228,050 spent on Radio and TV ads when these people have Radio/TV Marti for communications.

Orlando Gutiérrez National Secretary (salary $46,827) and Janniset Rivero Secretary (salary $48,203) are husband and wife. Vice President Lorenzo DeToro is Ms. Rivero's brother-in-law.

Source: Directorio Democratico IRS Form 990 for 2008, 2009, 2010

Foundation for Human Rights

	2008-2010
Total Income	$1,290,234
US Government	0
Fundraiser	$389,893
Telephone	$643
Website	$30,270
Travel	18,890
Assistance to Cuban Opposition Groups	$700,198

Percentage of income it claimed was dedicated to Assistance to Cuban Groups 42 percent. The key question however *is does that money go to Cuban Opposition Groups in Cuba, or some of the myriad Cuban Opposition Groups in Miami? And what has been the return on that money?*

Source: Foundation for Human Rights IRS Form 990 for 2008, 2009, 2010

One of the challenges of reviewing 990's is that there is no uniformity. Some are typed, others handwritten, and expenses are categorized differently. However the thing to point out is that somewhere there should be a substantial amount that has gone to Cuba, and that substantial amount is not present on any 990. In 2011, USAID announced that it was awarding a $3.4 Million grant to FHR over a three-year period. This caused an uproar among the Miami Cartel. South Florida Republican Rep. Mario Diaz-Balart complained that U.S. funds for democracy programs in Cuba 'should be provided only to organizations with strong experience and proven track records on the island.'

"It would be a disgrace if the Obama administration broke with tradition and used a penny of that critical funding to reward political cronies," Diaz-Balart added in an email. Mario Diaz-Belart likely would have preferred those funds go to his cronies in these shallow NGOs in which case some of the funds might have eventually ended up in his campaign coffers.

The following NGOs are listed in the 2011 USAID report along with a recap of the amounts they received. Commentary has been added for the reader's benefit.

Creative Associates received $7M from 8/2008 to 6/2012

No mention of Cuba on its website; no Cuba field office

Grupo de Apoyo a la Democracia received $75M from 10/2004 to 10/2008

No money in 2009; audit revealed purchase of crabmeat, chocolates, video games, cashmere sweaters and other items which do not help the people of Cuba. In 2008 claimed to have sent $835,345 in Humanitarian Aid to Cubans. Claimed that there were 500 beneficiaries; $1,670.69 average aid amount per recipient. This is a highly suspicious claim. Award reinstated - $1.5M from 9/2010 to 10/2012

International Relief & Development received $3.5M from 9/2011 to 9/2014

No mention of Cuba on website in projects or areas served

International Republican Institute received $3.7M from 8/2008 to 6/2012

Only mention of Cuba on website is links to news articles

Loyola University received $3M from 9/2010 through 9/2013

No mention of Cuba on website except for class listings

National Democratic Institute received $2.3M from 9/2011 through 9/2014

Only mention of Cuba on website is links to news articles

Pan-American Development Foundation receive $3.9M from 9/2011 to 9/2014

No dot for Cuba on website service area map; nor mention of Cuba at all on website

There is however *one group* which actually puts resources into helping the Cuban people:

ECHO Cuba has received $1M from 6/2009 to 6/2012

They are Christian-based and conduct mission trips to Cuba. Spent 5 percent on management; 2.1 percent on fundraising. Spent the balance on advocacy, community, and economic development in Cuba. Wonderful work by this group. God Bless them.

In Chapter 24 there was a reference to the Black Spring of 2003 when 75 human rights activists, independent journalists, and independent librarians were arrested by the Cuban government and sentenced up to 28 years in prison. One of the charges was accepting money from foreign governments, including the United States. It would seem that the Cuban government would be monitoring monies sent by remittance to certain individuals. Can anyone really verify if any of the $40+ Million pumped into the Miami Black Hole each year actually helps any Cuban people – in Cuba? In Miami?

More than $500 Million has been spent over the past decade by these and an assortment of other entities. Why so many groups? Every chieftain has to have his own kingdom, and has to put his queen and offspring on the payroll while taxpayers foot the bill. How much of these funds have funded terrorist operations? How much may have been used to support the comfortable South Florida lifestyle for terrorists who are protected and deified by terrorist collaborator Ileana Ros-Lehtinen.

The Miami Cartel enjoys riding this gravy train, and does not want to see it end soon or have any serious oversight. This means that the whole Cuban assistance program is wide open for abuse, fraud, and theft probably on a much greater scale than the crime of Felipe Sixto as detailed in the next chapter. An interesting exercise is to review Federal Election Commission campaign contribution reports and see the names of some employees of various entities who receive federal funds listed as contributors to Miami Cartel politicians.

When then Senator John Kerry questioned the effectiveness of these programs to State Department officials he was told that they were working and that they had 'trained hundreds of journalists.' There are roughly three dozen bloggers posting from inside Cuba. Where are the hundreds?

Cubans on the island who have been shown the IRS 990 and financial data of Grupo de Apoyo a la Democracia where Grupo claims to have sent $835,345 in grants to Cubans on the island with an average award of $1,670.69 have expressed shock and disbelief. These people earn less than $250 per year. Several have said, "For that kind of money given to my family, I would be willing to go to prison for accepting it."

Another reward waits for the person who can locate a Cuban citizen – activist, dissident, or ordinary citizen – who has received a financial grant from Grupo de Apoyo a la Democracia, or any other NGO. The 11 Million people of Cuba deserve better than these 'results' as do the taxpayers of the United States.

29. Felipe Sixto: Admitted Cuban Crook in the White House

The American public has long labeled elected officials and their lackeys and hangers-on as crooks. On Nov. 18, 1973, President Richard Nixon in a televised speech to the American people stated, "I am not a crook." Well there had been one bona fide crook of Miami Cartel heritage in the George W. Bush White House until he walked out the door on his way to federal prison.

Felipe Sixto[45] was Special Assistant to the President after coming to work at the White House from his position as chief of staff at the Center for a Free Cuba. While in that position he orchestrated a scam in which he incorporated a shell company to purchase portable radios from China. The shell company then resold the radios to his employer at an inflated price and it laundered the money through bogus bank accounts and P.O. boxes.

Sixto became so adept at his scam that when he left CFC and transitioned to the White House he kept it running. He set up new phony P. O. boxes and checking accounts. When CFC uncovered his scam and the US Justice Department began to pursue him, Sixto resigned from the Bush White House.

---

45   *washingtonpost.com/wpdyn/content/article/2009/03/18/AR2009031800661. html*

Asked about Sixto's resignation White House spokesman Scott Stanzel stated: "Mr. Sixto allegedly had a conflict of interest with the use of AID Funds."[46] An elaborate scheme which resulted in the theft of $579,274.47 by Mr. Sixto from US taxpayers was categorized as a conflict of interest by the White House. Sixto pled guilty and dragged out a cadre of people to plead for no prison time, to merely receive probation. With the help of his father he repaid the money he stole from CFC along with interest totaling $644,844.60.

Sixto appealed to the US District Court judge for leniency and home confinement saying he had concocted his scheme because he 'wanted to provide a lifestyle for my family I could not afford.' The judge compared him to Bernie Madoff and said that Sixto like Madoff wanted a lifestyle 'far above' what he deserved. The judge sentenced Sixto to two-and-a-half years in prison and a $10,000 fine.

The Cuban media refers to the Miami Cartel in elected and appointed power or positions of authority as the "Miami Mafia." With its various tentacles, hands, and fingers in so many interests that is a good analogy. One might suspect that with all the money floating around and with all the cross-breeding and nepotism in these groups that Felipe Sixto is not the only crook, he is just the only one who got caught.

When news of Sixto's crime broke, CFC Executive Director Frank Calzon said he felt a 'personal betrayal' by his protégé and expressed outrage over the situation in interviews with various Miami media. Calzon stated that the scam that Sixto pulled related to short wave radios purchased from China then reshipped to Cuba for distribution. Calzon claimed that using US taxpayer money he had shipped 30,000 radios to Cuba from 1998 to 2007.

In a heated Spanish televised debate on May 22, 2007 in which Calzon participated with Miami Democratic Chairman Joe Garcia, the chairman pointed out that it costs three times as much to ship a radio to Cuba as to just send the money and let the Cubans buy their own. Calzon stated that Cubans are not

---

46   cubamcud.org/English/News/News201.htm

allowed to buy radios. If what Calzon says is true that Cubans cannot buy radios is it not a stretch to believe him that he could ship in 30,000 without the Cuban government noticing?

Let's deal first things first. Cubans can in fact buy radios, because during blackouts they would die without being able to at least listen to their beloved baseball on a battery operated radio.

Second, a person owning one laptop, one iPad, one cell phone, and one iPod should not have problems getting through Havana customs. But if they carry donations of used cell phones to give to families during mission trips or flash drives to give to college students, their items will be scrutinized. Multiple cell phones will cause their bag to be searched and they have to explain the gifts. This is a byproduct of the Alan Gross arrest and conviction.

So it is very difficult to believe that anyone, not even the pope himself, could get 30,000 radios into Cuba. In parishes across the island, never has a hand gone up when a group was asked if they'd ever been given a radio.

Another reward awaits the person who can locate a short-wave radio sent since 1998 by the Center for a Free Cuba to anyone in Cuba. If 30,000 radios were shipped into the country, the Cuban citizens deserve to have access to them.

30. Miami - Deadbeat Dad Capital of America

The conversation is the same, and can take place on any day, in any Cuban city, with a young man or lady.

Visitor: *Very nice to meet you. So where are you from?*

Cuban: *Well I live here in Havana but I was born in Cienfuegos. My family still lives there.*

Visitor: *Oh, do you get back to Cienfuegos to visit often?*

Cuban: *Yes I go visit my family once a month.*

Visitor: *So who do you have back home for family?*

Cuban: *My mother, my brother, my sister and her husband, my grandmother, and my uncle.*

Visitor: *And how about your father, is he still alive?*

Cuban: *Yes, he is in the United States.*

Visitor: *In Miami?*

Cuban: *Yes, how did you know? He has been there five years.*

Visitor: *Why do you not go there and live with him?*

Cuban: *My father says it is very complicated; maybe two or three more years he brings me there.*

The Cuban lobby in Congress has among other amoral things aided and abetted hundreds of Cuban men in their efforts to abandon their children emotionally and financially by coming to the US and ignoring their family back home.

Cubans hear rumors from friends about the process of obtaining a visa to emigrate to the United States. They rely however on their parents or other relative in the US, feeling they would not be deceived. But the truth is not what many young people are told.

In November 2007 the Department of Homeland Security established the Cuban Family Reunification Parole (CFRP) Program. The plan allows approved family members of legal US residents to come to the United States rather than wait in Cuba to apply for a green card. The program is designed to expedite family reunification through an orderly method and to discourage dangerous and irregular maritime migration.

Although there is no specific timeline the completion of this process should be expeditious. The U.S.-based petitioner submits paperwork and when the paperwork review is completed the petitioner then calls to set an interview appointment in Havana. If the interview is a success the émigré will receive their approval in approximately one month.

If this information could be disseminated widely in Cuba more young people might clamor to come join their parents. This is even more probable now since the Cuban 'exit visa' has gone away as of January 12, 2013. More information on CFRP is available at havana.usint.gov.

Another boon to the Deadbeat Cuban Dads who have abandoned their families has been the remittance guidelines. During the Bush administration family remittance levels were cut to $300 per quarter. A person flying back to visit family in Cuba could only carry $300. Visits back home were limited to once every three years. This gave Deadbeat Cuban Dads the cover they needed. When their children in Cuba asked them to send more money they could cite the fact that the US government would only allow them to send $1,200 per year. After taking office in 2009 President Obama eliminated the limits on family remittances. He also instituted a policy of allowing people to send remittances of up to $500 per quarter to non-family members.

The Cubans in Congress were irate over this decision by President Obama to help improve the lives of families in Cuba.

This unlimited remittance to families had to anger some Miami Cartel if their families back home learned of the change and began asking for more money. In one of the Miami Cartel blogs the Mitt Romney agenda for Cuba was articulated should he have won the 2012 presidential election. First and foremost he would have demanded unilaterally that Alan Gross be returned with no consideration. Not ask, demand. Good luck with that, Governor.

Romney also stated he would have eliminated the People-to-People travel programs which were expanded by President Obama. Most important and most detrimental to families in Cuba his platform stated that he would have reduced the family remittance limits to Bush 2004 limits and eliminate the remittance provisions for non-relatives. He would have also returned to only one visit back to family in Cuba every three years. Fortunately for the people of Cuba, Mitt Romney lost the election.

If the Cuban government wanted to wreak havoc and put a huge strain on South Florida's judicial and school systems it could arrange transportation for anyone under the age of 18 whose father is living in Miami, via a cruise ship or other large vessel. Let these kids hit the Florida shores and head to the court-house to file paternity suits and claims for back due child support. Then let them register in the public schools and overwhelm them. Children in Cuba deserve the full financial support of their US-protected parents. There should be some mechanism to require Deadbeat Cuban Dads in the US to financially support their children back home.

31. Rafael Diaz Balart – the Original Spin Doctor

There is probably no person who played a greater role in painting a negative picture for the US Senate in 1960 of his ex-brother-in-law Fidel Castro than Rafael Lincoln Diaz-Balart, former Deputy Minister of the brutal Interior Ministry in the Batista Dictatorship.

On May 3, 1960 Diaz-Balart testified before the *US Senate Subcommittee to Investigate the Administration of the Internal Security Act and Other Internal Security Laws, of the Committee on the Judiciary in a hearing on 'The Communist Threat to the United States through the Caribbean'*. The hearing was convened by Senator Thomas Dodd.[47]

Diaz-Balart testified about how he came to be in the United States. "I left Cuba, on December 20, 1958, to Europe, for some professional business, find while there the Communist forces of Castro arrived to power, so I remained there until January 15 when I came here, to the United States."

Notwithstanding the fact that most of professional Europe at that time shut down for Christmas on December 15, and the fact that he had brought his entire family along on this business trip, Diaz-Balart was truly blessed to have fled Cuba 8 days before the start of the Battle of Santa Clara and 12 days before his patron Fulgencio Batista fled Cuba for the Dominican Republic with $300 Million.

---

47   *latinamericanstudies.org/us-cuba/diaz-balart.htm*

Diaz-Balart claimed New York Times reporter Herbert Matthews was responsible for Castro's popularity because Matthews had written an article about Castro and his rebels at their camp in the Sierra Maestra Mountains.

Much of his testimony is convoluted and in some cases he contradicts himself but the spinning is obvious. He downplayed the brutality of the Batista Dictatorship of which he had been a part as Deputy Minister of the Interior and congressman. He made no mention of Batista's death squads executing 20,000 people, in spite of those executions coming under the auspices of the Interior Ministry of which Diaz-Balart had intimate knowledge as its former Deputy Minister.[48]

Diaz-Balart did not mention that Frank Pais, a 23 year old teacher who had been recruiting for the rebels was captured and tortured to death by agents of Batista's Interior Ministry on a public street in Santiago on March 11, 1957.[49]

Diaz-Balart did not mention that Batista had ordered Captain Esteban Venture of his police to shoot to death four student leaders in an apartment at 7 Humboldt Street in Havana in what is now known as the 7 Humboldt Street Massacre.[50]

Diaz-Balart did not mention that Batista had set up the first 'public-private partnership' for property development. $14 Million of public funds in Cuba went to build the Riviera Hotel and then ownership of the property was turned over to US mobster Myer Lansky.

What Diaz-Balart did testify to endlessly was Fidel and Raul Castro's supposed affiliation with the Communist Party. Given the times and the topic of the hearing, this was probably a good way he could ingratiate himself with the senators. Diaz-Balart also warned that Castro might send agitators to some states in the South which would exacerbate 'the Negro problem' in the United States. In addition to everything else it seems that Rafael

48   Conflict, Order, and Peace in the Americas, by the Lyndon B. Johnson School of Public Affairs, 1978, pg 121 ~ "The US-supported Batista regime killed 20,000 Cubans"

49   books.google.com/books?id=tYtuZj7A940C&pg=PA69&lpg=PA69&dq=batista +humboldt+street+massacre

50   books.google.com/books?id=tYtuZj7A940C&pg=PA69&lpg=PA69&dq=batista +humboldt+street+massacre

Lincoln Diaz-Balart was a racist, which made him well-suited to be part of the Batista Dictatorship.

Rafael Diaz-Balart never uttered a negative word about the dictator Fulgencio Batista; in fact he came off as an apologist for the brutal tyrant. He did however use the word 'communist' 71 times while referring to Fidel and Raul Castro.

Diaz-Balart also testified that in the 1940's while they were students at the University of Havana (and when he introduced Fidel to his sister, and Fidel's future wife) Fidel shot and killed two fellow students. These assassinations according to Diaz-Balart in separate incidents occurred in the open around the University, one in the middle of the street. Then, according to Diaz-Balart Castro shot and killed a sergeant of the university police 'because the sergeant had told that he was going to put Fidel in jail because of the previous killing.'(sic) None of these supposed killings have ever been verified by any source, in spite of them having taken place in broad daylight by a university campus.

In describing one of the killings Diaz-Balart testified about Castro coming to him before the murder: "He invited me to participate with him in the killing of that student, and I refused, because I am a Christian, I am against killing, and besides that, there was not any reason to." Yet if he is to be believed, Rafael Diaz-Balart allowed his sister to marry a cold blooded murderer with three notches in his gun belt. He was some brother.

Approximately five years later in 1952, Diaz-Balart was Deputy Minister in Batista's Interior Ministry. MININT oversaw kidnapping, rape, torture, and executions by firing squad of people for whom there was probably not any reason to kill, save for their opposition to the Batista Dictatorship. Whether Diaz-Balart lost his Christianity or his opposition to killing is open to speculation. In time his organization La Blanca Rosa (the white rose) and hundreds like it that were formed in the United States and continued to twist and spin the facts and control the message about Fidel Castro and his Cuban government. These groups also engaged in terroristic activities in the United States. (See Appendix A)

A further question is this: since he held a Deputy Minister's position and then a congressman's position in the Batista Dictatorship, why did Rafael Diaz-Balart not seek the prosecution of Fidel Castro for the three murders Castro allegedly committed in 1947? He could have provided first hand testimony and helped get Castro convicted and imprisoned. Cuba and the world would have never heard of Fidel Castro. He was a powerful man in the Interior Ministry; he could have had Castro killed by one of the Ministry's firing squads. His biography claims he made an 'impassioned speech' in the Cuban Congress opposing the clemency of the Castro Brothers in 1955. He warned of what they would do if freed from prison. Why did he not speak about these horrible murders he would eventually testify about before the United States Senate?

Mr. Diaz-Balart has gone on to his final reward, so the veracity of those murder accusations or any of that testimony will never be known.

The Diaz-Balart spin continues to this day, emanating from the sons of Rafael Diaz-Balart and from the Miami Cartel. These people have had an inordinate amount of influence and assistance in helping to keep their 11Million countrymen down. In a *New York Times* interview in 2006 Lincoln Diaz-Balart boasted that he was batting 1.000 in controlling the Bush Administration's policies toward his Uncle Fidel's Cuba.[51] He also denied claims that he wants to go and succeed his uncle as leader of Cuba if the country opens up, claiming he just wants democratic elections. It is difficult to believe that someone who comes from a family that was so enmeshed in the Batista Dictatorship and had made every effort to deny improved quality of life for the Cuban people would want democracy. Lincoln Diaz-Balart also stated that he had written the Helms-Burton Act when it is widely known that it was written by the legal counsel for the Bacardi Rum family.

In discussing his opposition to Cuba participating in the World Baseball Classic in the US with the *New York Times*, Lincoln Diaz-Balart stated, "You have invited a totalitarian dictatorship which has murdered thousands and imprisoned hundreds of thousands for the 'crime' of supporting freedom and democracy."

---

51   *nytimes.com/2006/03/08/national/08miami.html?_r=0*

Thousands murdered? I've met hundreds of Cubans who have spoken with me openly and I have never had someone tell me a loved one was one of thousands killed. Hundreds of thousands imprisoned? Seriously, Lincoln? Cuba only has 545 prisons, some as small as twenty cells.[52] If just 100,000 were truly imprisoned, that would be an average 1835 prisoners per institution. Considering that during the 1980 Mariel Boatlift Castro emptied all his prisons and shipped inmates to the US (remember Scarface[53]) 'hundreds of thousands' is probably a gross exaggeration. But the Diaz-Balart brothers continue to spin the narrative about their uncle Fidel, carrying on their father's legacy of distortion. This family feud makes the McCoys and Hatfields look tame.

In November, 2012, Mario Diaz-Balart and Ileana Ros Lehtinen called on the Obama Administration to immediately deport a Cuban refugee, Crescencio Marina Rivero who had been an official in the Cuban Interior Ministry under Castro. Diaz-Balart as usual said nothing worth quoting. Ros-Lehtinen stated, "It is the height of hypocrisy for this former official of the feared and brutal Cuban Ministry of the Interior (MININT) to spend his golden years in the comfort and freedom Miami offers."[54] Those very same words could have been spoken in 1959 about Rafael Lincoln Diaz-Balart, former official of the feared and brutal Cuban MININT.

The building that houses the Florida International University College of Law bears his name, 'Rafael Diaz-Balart Hall.' Until his death he stated he would not return to his homeland unless Castro had been driven from power. Cubans will tell you that if he ever had come home he would have faced a myriad of criminal charges from his days as Deputy Interior Minister, and a likely death sentence.

The expression 'the tail is wagging the dog' is appropriate here because it is visually palpable. The whole of the United States is the dog, and Florida the tail that has wagged the country and driven a policy towards Cuba that runs contrary to everything the United States stands for, and that has hurts 11 Million people for 54 years.

---

52   cubaverdad.net/list_prisons_in_cuba.htm
53   en.wikipedia.org/wiki/Scarface_(1983_film)
54   mariodiaz-balart.house.gov/press-releases/diazbalart-and-roslehtinen-request-expulsion-of-former-regime-enforcer-living-in-the-us/

The complete transcript of Rafael Diaz-Balart's 1960 Senate testimony is included in Appendix B

The Batista Dictatorship – overseers of torture, kidnapping, sexual assault, and murder, reportedly killed 20,000 opponents and dissidents. Some were killed by firing squad. Others were gunned down on the street; a group of four college students were massacred by Batista's police in an apartment.

Rafael Lincoln Diaz Balart (center with holstered pistol)who served as one of Batista's Deputy Ministers of the Interior pictured with the Masferrer Brothers, two of Batista's goons. Older Cubans recount tales of their alleged brutality. The building that houses the Law School at Florida International University is named after Rafael Lincoln Diaz-Balart.

32. Enablers of Terror in Congress

Through the years Congress has had its share of ethically challenged and questionable characters. Some have been expelled from the house; others have gone to prison. Yet there currently sits in the US House of Representatives from the 18th District of Florida a woman who through her entire career as a federal lawmaker has figuratively been in bed with and given aid and comfort to two of the most dangerous terrorists in the Western Hemisphere.

That person is terrorist collaborator Ileana Ros-Lehtinen, daughter of the terrorist sympathizer Enrique Ros. Ileana Ros-Lehtinen has figuratively urinated on the Flag of the United States of America in the US Capitol. She has taken the American Flag and wrapped it around dangerous murdering terrorists and protected them in her Miami lair. Enrique Ros collaborated with one of his daughter's beloved terrorists on a 1994 revisionist history of the Bay of Pigs invasion. Ros-Lehtinen and her father are tightly intertwined with the Miami Cartel terrorist community.[55]

Since her arrival in the US House in 1989 Ros-Lehtinen has been the terrorists' best friend in Congress. Some older Cubans nickname her "Mama Ros' after the legendary American crime matron Ma Barker. When terrorist Orlando Bosch was arrested in

---

55   wikispooks.com/wiki/Ileana Ros-Lehtinen

Miami for parole violations and faced deportation Ros-Lehtinen intervened via her campaign manager Jeb Bush. Jeb got his father President George H.W. Bush to give Bosch a pardon by fiat. During the time she was lobbying for the convicted terrorist's pardon she even organized an *Orlando Bosch Day* in Miami an event to celebrate the murders of innocent adults and children.

In 2000, she led the charge of the Miami Cartel seeking to steal Elian Gonzalez from his father in what became a world-wide fiasco played out on American television. That fever pitch hatred carried over into the trial of the Cuban Five.

Ros-Lehtinen has defended former fugitive Velentin Hernández, convicted of murdering Luciano Nieves, a fellow Cuban exile that supported negotiations with the Cuban government.[56] She was referred to in a conversation as 'La Cochino' (The Pig) by a member of Los Damas de Blanco, a nickname used by ordinary Cubans who despise this cartoonish self-proclaimed Freedom Fighter.

Overall, Ros-Lehtinen has managed for more than two decades to mislead members of Congress and the public at large as to what has been happening in Cuba. It has been her spin, much to the detriment of 11 Million people. She claims to care about dissidents in Cuba but it appears she sees them merely as talking points.

Many Cuban citizens believe Ros-Lehtinen may have had involvement in the planning of the bombing of the tourist sites in Havana in 1997. The bombings were financed by Jorge Mas Canosa and carried out by Ros' terrorist soulmate Luis Posada and his Salvadoran associates. She was very determined trying to shut down an FBI investigation in Havana of the bombings. She has never expressed one word of distaste or condemnation of any act perpetrated by the various Miami Cartel terrorist groups against any civilian target in Cuba or the United States. She was AWOL in April 2012 when one of her constituent's travel agency in Coral Gables was bombed, one month after booking 310 people to Havana to see Pope Benedict XVI.

---

56 *articles.nydailynews.com/1999-09-12/news/18122639_1_ clemency-offer-mrs-clinton-puerto-rican-nationalists*

A true man of God in Cuba is Jaime Cardinal Ortega Alamino, the leader of the Catholic Church in Cuba. The Cardinal was jailed for three years in the 1960s for celebrating masses after religion had been banned. Today he has a strong relationship with the Castro brothers, yet walks a fine line balancing the church's mission and the Cuban government edicts.

He has brought both Pope John Paul II and Pope Benedict XVI to Cuba. He has forged a respect with the Castros that enabled him to negotiate for the release of almost 3,000 prisoners in December 2011. The terrorist collaborator Ros-Lehtinen has spoken of the Cardinal in contemptuous terms calling him a 'Castro collaborator.' How crass for this amoral woman to speak this way of Cardinal Ortega. He has done more for Cuban political prisoners than the cartoonish self-proclaimed 'freedom fighter' ever has.

After the Florida GOP presidential primary debate in Tampa on Jan. 24, 2012 where the GOP candidates came to cozy up to the Miami Cartel, two candidates mentioned Ros-Lehtinen as a potential cabinet member. When asked what role she would like in a Romney administration, she replied, "Ambassador to a free Cuba."

There are many ordinary citizens in Cuba who would like to see the terrorist sympathizer Ros-Lehtinen on the island so they could call her to task for her terrorist alliances and for the alleged sins of her father. Drop her name in Havana before a group of Biki cab drivers who are screaming at one another arguing about baseball and immediately they will all get on the same page: welcoming her with machetes if she ever sets foot in the country. It's stunning – as despised as Hillary Clinton and Sarah Palin are in some quarters, I've never heard groups of men fantasizing about bringing about their demise. It shows the level of hatred that Cubans have for this woman who would have the White House and Congress believe that she is a 'freedom fighter' with wide support in her native country.

In March, 2013 Ros-Lehtinen criticized the Castro government for the alleged beating of a rights protester in Santa Clara. Ros-Lehtinen piled on with criticism of the Obama Administration saying they give "More diplomatic entreaties and concessions to this vile and ruthless octogenarian clique of despots that has turned Cuba into an economic and social basket case." With that description she could have been talking about her father Enrique, her terrorist soulmate Luis Posada and their allies who never quite made it to octogenarian status, Jorge Mas Canosa and Orlando Bosch.

If that beating did in fact take place, as it was not mentioned on any of the Cuban activist blogs, the best way to prevent such incidents from occurring is to have a sea of sneakers on the streets in Cuba, to have so many that no government agents would ever act out of turn in front of dozens of tourist cameras. But for 'La Cochino' Ros-Lehtinen, squealing and complaining about something is much more politically satisfying than trying to eliminate the problem. In American politics the controversial issues never get resolved: abortion, gun safety, etc. because they are cash cows for politicians. In Miami the cash cow is the Castro Brothers. Why would Ros-Lehtinen, Diaz-Balart and their terrorist allies want to see improved relations with Cuba? It might expose some of their families' dirty secrets, and dry up their source of campaign cash.

The other supporters of terrorism in the U.S House have been Congressman Mario Diaz-Balart, his brother former Congressman Lincoln Diaz-Balart, and former Congressman David Rivera. The Diaz-Balarts are the nephews of Fidel Castro.

Their father was interior minister in the Batista Dictatorship and later a congressman as noted in Chapter 31. Lest anyone confuse Cuba's interior ministry with the US Department of the Interior they could not be more different. The US Department of the Interior deals with national parks, etc. The Cuban Interior Ministry dealt with the military, national police, firing squads, and during the Batista Dictatorship, torture, and the kidnapping of young school girls who were to be put in service at the brothels run by the US Mafia.

The Diaz-Balarts are Fidel Castro's nephews by marriage – Rafael's sister Mirta was Fidel's first wife. There is talk around

Miami that the Diaz-Balarts feel that with Jorge Mas Canosa dead they are heirs apparent to go to Cuba and take over the government when Fidel Castro dies. In Cuba the Diaz-Balart brothers are known as Coco y Loco – Dumb and Dumber. They and Ileana Ros-Lehtinen collectively are referred to as 'Los Tres Chiflados' – the Three Stooges.

David Rivera's character shortcomings are well documented in the *Miami Herald* archives as well as his Wikipedia page including allegations of domestic violence, ongoing FBI and IRS investigations, and questionable financial dealings involving his mother and a political consultant. Rivera is living testament to the fact that Cuban-Floridians are gullible and believe what they are told by Miami Cartel leaders: if they 'don't elect a Cubano we may lose all our rights.' Hence they will vote for anyone with Cuban roots regardless of how morally barren he may be.

The one-term House member introduced a bill HR2831 to modify the Cuban Adjustment Act to revoke permanent residency status from any Cuban immigrant who returns home to visit family in Cuba before they receive permanent citizenship

Rivera accused many immigrants of gaming the system since the Obama administration relaxed the rules on family travel in 2009: coming here to obtain benefits then going back and forth to spend it living the high life in Cuba. He made the somewhat dubious claim that this has cost US taxpayers billions that have gone to Cuba. If this is truly the case, then why not suspend all these taxpayer handouts to Cuban immigrants? Mexican, Guatemalan, and Salvadoran immigrants don't receive such benefits, nor do immigrants from Iraq, Iran, Afghanistan, Rwanda, or Myanmar. Why should Cubans?

On the Senate side is Marco Rubio, Tea Party darling and potential 2016 GOP presidential nominee. His two claims to fame are his misuse of a Florida GOP credit card for personal expenses when he was Speaker of the Florida House,[57] and lying about his

---

57   *tampabay.com/news/politics/legislature/article1075692.ece*

family's history.[58] On the stump as he rose through various political ranks, Rubio, the former staff member to Ros-Lehtinen, would tell groups while campaigning how his parents had fled the tyranny of Castro's Cuba. The problem is that his father already was working at a job in Miami in 1956 and Castro did not come to power until 1959.

Reading the details of Rubio's credit card issues along with PACs he created, the details are reminiscent of the NGOs profiled in Chapter 28. Family members put on payrolls, personal expenses for food, auto repairs, ten airline tickets for a young female healthcare lobbyist . . . it goes on and on. Rather than put a footnote here, the actual link to the full Mother Jones article about Rubio is here: motherjones.com/politics/2012/04/ten-things-you-need-know-about-marco-rubio

In February 2103 Rubio gave a speech before an anti-Castro PAC in Washington, DC and criticized both People-to-People programs and his Senate colleagues for traveling to Cuba. "Cuba is not a zoo, where you get to pay for admission and watch people living in cages," proclaimed the Senator.

Senator, Cuba is in fact a zoo as a result of the belligerent and anti-Christian attitude of you and the other members of the Miami Cartel. You have put them in enclosures by refusing to allow them to travel to the United States. Raul Castro eliminated exit visas this year; so now the US is the only country in the world to which Cubans cannot travel freely. You are really an advocate for your people aren't you, Senator Rubio?

Senator Bob Menendez, (D-NJ) touts the Cuban immigrant line railing against Fidel Castro when he can as noted previously in Chapter 3. As of this writing in March 2013, Menendez is under FBI investigation along with one of his super-contributors, a Florida doctor.

It was learned that Menendez flew twice to the Dominican Republic on the doctor's private jet and had not reported it on his financial disclosure form. So to 'clear up the clerical error by his staff' he wrote a $58,000 check from his personal funds. It's easy

58   washingtonpost.com/politics/marco-rubios-compelling-family-story-embellishes-facts-documents-show/2011/10/20/gIQAaVHD1L_story.html

to see why the senator has difficulty relating to people who make $20 per month.

The newest politician on the national scene with Cuban blood in his veins is Canada native Ted Cruz, Republican Senator from Texas. Cruz misled voters of Texas by running ads claiming that his father escaped tyranny and torture in Cuba. Problem with that storyline is that depending on the version you hear from Cruz and his supporters perhaps his father fought tyranny and torture by the Batista Dictatorship right alongside Fidel Castro. That he was captured and tortured by the Batista Dictatorship, then given a student visa by Batista to come to Texas.[59] Or maybe he escaped Castro's Cuba and torture because he spoke out against Castro. Cruz shares as little as possible about his father's alliances in Cuba as he does about the fact that he is a Canadian native. The Cuban-American politicians have a wide open path to deception because records in Cuba cannot be accessed and any talk of torture to an American audience with a limited knowledge of world events immediately conjures up the man Republicans love to hate, Fidel Castro.

Cruz arrived in the Senate in January 2013 and immediately sought to steal the limelight. He attacked then Secretary of State Hillary Clinton during the Benghazi Hearings and assailed the character of former Senator Chuck Hagel during his confirmation hearings for Secretary of Defense. The he attacked President Obama's support for immigration reform claiming the president wanted the legislation 'to crater.' His attacks were so bad that even senators from his own party castigated him publicly. Of course Cruz, like Rubio, comes from the Tea Party, though Cruz seems to be more aligned with the loose cannon wing. He is a Harvard educated lawyer who has acted like a fool in his first months in the Senate.

Plenty can be ascertained about all these characters via Internet searches. One fact about all of them stands out: since April 25, 2012 the day the offices of Cuban travel arranger Airline Brokers in Coral Gables was bombed, the agency which booked

---

59   trailblazersblog.dallasnews.com/2011/10/ted-cruz-background-as-son-of.html/

310 people to Cuba for the Papal Masses, not one of the so-called law-and-order types in the Miami Cartel uttered one word of consolation, disgust, or anger. And that omission speaks volumes about the character of the Miami Cartel politicians who idolize terrorists while lacking moral compasses.

Just as this book was going to press, word came that the entertainers Jay-Z and Beyoncé had spent several days in Havana celebrating their fifth wedding anniversary. With problems in Iraq, Afghanistan, Libya, Syria, Egypt, Somalia, and with North Korea threatening to fire nuclear missiles at the US, what did terrorist collaborator Ileana Ros-Lehtinen and her terrorist ally Mario Diaz-Balart demand from the White House? An investigation into whether or not the two has a travel license. Jay-Z raised money for Obama's campaign; Beyoncé famously lip-synched the National Anthem at President Obama's Inauguration. Oh my gosh! They must be Fascist Communists down there plotting with Raul Castro. Get FOX News on the case.

Showing just how ignorant and ill-informed she is, Ros-Lehtinen went on a rant that the couple had spent money with the regime. The couple dined at private, non-government restaurants such as La Guarida. If Ros-Lehtinen were to visit Cuba – in spite of being Public Enemy #2 she would see that the tired old lies she and her fellow Cartel members spread through the years are just that – lies.

President George W. Bush said in 2003, "If you support a terrorist, you're a terrorist." Well if that is true then the Congress of the United States has at least one terrorist among its membership. The lead terrorist in Congress, by George W. Bush's standard would be Florida's Ileana Ros-Lehtinen with a 22 year history of protecting and supporting terrorists.

Congresswoman Ileana Ros-Lehtinen Republican of Florida came to Congress in 1989 upon the death of Claude Pepper. In 1990 she began her legacy of giving aid and comfort to terrorists. She is the first known terrorist in Congress as defined by President George W. Bush and the first terrorist to Chair the House Committee on Foreign Affairs. She is considered Public Enemy #2 in Cuba, after her terrorist soul-mate Luis Posada Carilles.

In his 2002 State of the Union address, President Bush identified countries he claimed constituted an 'axis of evil.' Those countries were Iraq, Iran, and North Korea and President Bush said the United States faced threats from each one of them.[60]

In May of that year, Undersecretary of State John Bolton spoke at an event sponsored by the Heritage Foundation. He expanded the axis of evil to include Libya, Syria, and Cuba.[61]

Adding Cuba to that group is like adding Austin Powers' 'Mini-Me' to a National Basketball Association lineup. Yes Cuba had given safe haven to members of the Columbian group FARC, but we've given haven in Miami to terrorists who've killed more innocent people than FARC. And more important, Cuba had never perpetrated any act of terror against the US.

---

60   presidency.ucsb.edu/ws/index.php?pid=29644
61   heritage.org/research/lecture/beyond-the-axis-of-evil

The designation as a 'state sponsor of terrorism' remains. This requires any citizen of Cuba wishing to travel to the United States to be interviewed by State Department personnel at the US Interests Section. The State Department's website as of March 2013 says that the wait time for an appointment is over one year.[62] So much for "Give me your tired, your poor, your huddled masses yearning to breathe free." This designation should be removed immediately. In 2008 the Bush Administration removed North Korea from the list and as this is being written the country's Supreme Leader Kim Jong Un is threatening to launch nuclear missiles against the United States.

On January 12, 2013 in the latest reforms announced by President Raul Castro exit visa requirements were eliminated for Cubans, as well as the requirement that they have a documented invitation to visit another country. Cubans are now free to travel to almost anywhere in the free world. The exception: the United States. With the state sponsor of terrorism label on Cuba, their citizens must still be interviewed by State Department person-nel. The Miami Cartel is fighting any suggestion that Secretary of State John Kerry may remove the designation, allowing Cubans to travel freely to the United States. If these charlatans in Miami really cared about the Cuban people they would push to make travel easier for them.

Why the Miami Cartel can hold sway claiming to 'speak for the people of Cuba' is stupefying. Every one of their actions has been to the detriment of their fellow Cubans. They all speak as experts yet none of them have ever been to the country, save for Ileana Ros-Lehtinen who was last there at age 8 when her father fled the crackdown of Batista loyalists.

Haven't we been down this route before in international poli-tics? Before the 2003 invasion of Iraq, the US Government was led down the path of WMD's by another world class fraud, Ahmed Shalabi. We gave millions to his government in exile and when it was time to send him into Iraq to lead the country he was wanted for crimes in several other countries.

---

62   *havana.usint.gov/visa_appointment_information.html*

As a final point in this chapter, mention has to be made of legendary major league baseball manager Ozzie Gillen of the Miami Marlins. In April 2012 *Time Magazine* posted comments on its website from Guillen. In making reference to Castro's longevity in power Guillen said "I love Castro." He wasn't professing a romantic devotion to the man he was just using a variation of an American euphemism. ("Ya gotta love so-and-so because he...") It is a rather sarcastic expression, generally used in describing scoundrels.

The Miami Cartel and the Cuban-Floridian community went ballistic. They marched on Marlins Stadium in the days prior to its grand opening demanding Guillen be fired. The hatred that permeates these people is truly sickening. Imagine what they could accomplish if they put that energy into something positive, like helping people back home in Cuba?

Marlins management caved in to pressure from the Miami Cartel and suspended Guillen without pay for five games. Then they announced that they would make a $150,000 donation to a group working for human rights in Cuba. More money to be scammed and more money to be funneled into political campaign coffers. It is a safe bet that none of that $150,000 made it to Cuba. What a shame the money wasn't donated to the Caritas Catholic Charity which does stellar work in Cuba.

The Miami Cartel calls to mind an organized crime syndicate; murder, money, harassment, protection, shakedown and coercion, forced loyalty, and criminal hierarchy. The early refugees from Cuba were the dregs: remnants of the Batista Dictatorship – a crime syndicate that Fidel Castro broke up. There were criminals: hoodlums, thugs, pimps, rapists, kidnappers, and assorted other nefarious characters. They transposed their actions and behavior onto Castro and his people and portrayed themselves as victims and the American people bought it. And they have been buying it for 54 years.

Section IV.
The Cuban
Healthcare System

33. The Miracle at CIREN

The low point of my life over the past several years was receiving a diagnosis of Early Onset Alzheimer's Disease. Especially troubling was being told that the only pharmaceuticals available were designed to manage the symptoms. There are no drugs available in the US to stem the progression of this disease or to even slow it down.

I've come to realize that in this country, emphasis is placed not on curing diseases but on managing the ailments with pharmaceuticals. I now cringe when I hear about a Walk/Run/Ride/Swim for the Cure. Hundreds of thousands of Americans take part in these fundraisers every year under the misconception that the entity is working on a cure. There is no money in curing diseases, and Big Pharma views every patient with any long-term or fatal disease as a revenue stream.

When my condition got to a point that I had to 'come out' so to speak, I shared the news with my circle of friends including on Facebook. Several friends that I'd made in Cuba who work in healthcare reached out and said, "Paul you need to come to CIREN[63] in Cuba."

CIREN is a Spanish acronym that translates to International Center for Neurological Restoration. I applied for admission and

---

63   www.ciren.cu/

was accepted as the first US citizen to be treated, and the first patient with Early Onset. With the support of friends in Mexico and Argentina and the love of my Cuban friends, I headed to CIREN for five weeks. My treatment and therapy was five full days and a half-day on Saturday. Saturday afternoon I would head with my assistant to a parish in the Archdiocese of Havana to share fellowship with parishioners and attend Sunday mass among them.

The proof is in the pudding as they say and here are the results of my test scores on arrival at CIREN and pre-departure.

Verbal & Semantic fluency: My F score went from 5 to 26; my A score went from 12 to 28, and my S score went from 11 to 31.

I won't get into the boring details of these scores but it is obvious that I made tremendous progress. In addition I had developed a severe stutter which is a rare symptom of Early Onset. My therapy and treatment eliminated my stutter. For more details on my scores as well as video of my 'before and after' visit my blog paulzheimers.blogspot.com

The medical staffs at CIREN, from doctors to nurses and therapists were truly amazing and dedicated. Each morning my treatment team of 12 people would visit me in my room at my patient house. The Spanish culture of hugs and kisses on the cheek was prevalent. When I had my MRI a nurse stood on either side of my gurney holding my hand and stroking my arm to keep me calm.

On my last day at CIREN I took my entire treatment team to lunch, something that had never taken place. I told them in my farewell remarks that my success was due 20 percent to medications, 30 percent to therapies, and 50 percent to their love and support. I know that we have many loving and dedicated healthcare workers here in the US. Unfortunately they are employed by for-profit corporations and can't take the time to give such personal attention to their patients.

My Alzheimer's wasn't cured at CIREN, but I created an analogy to illustrate what took place. I imagine that I am in a football game and on the opponent's 35-yard line headed towards the end zone. But in the case of Alzheimer's this end zone is terminal. The treatment at CIREN pushed me back across the 50-yard line likely all the way to my own 20. That beats a simple daily pill.

My heart is forever indebted to my treatment team, and to my friends in Mexico and Argentina for their loving support and assistance.

Every morning my Treatment Team would come to my patient house at 8:00 am for a review and preview of my activities

My two heroines at CIREN: Yohandra my speech therapist (logopedia) and Lena my orientation therapist (rehabilitator)

Section V.
Closing

34. Tourism, Entrepreneurship, and a Seawall

Ileana Ros-Lehtinen claims it should be criminal for tourists to be giving hard currency to the Castro regime. But the Cuban tourism industry is overwhelmingly populated by independent small businesses. Casa Particulars all across the country, hundreds in Havana alone, with clean accommodations for $20-$40 per night per room. There are hundreds of private car owners willing to drive you across town or across the country separate from the government run Cuba Taxi. Various food outlets – small 'cafeterias' operated out of a window in a home to well-appointed sit down restaurants – all are all privately owned. My favorite private restaurant in Havana is La Ros Negro. Five people can have a first-class meal there with beverages for under $35.

Follow the trail of this 1 CUC in the hands of a tourist, an example of what is known in economics as the multiplier effect:

Buy disposable razor from street vendor 1 CUC > street vendor buys coffee and roll from baker > baker buys sandwich from cafeteria > cafeteria owner buys beer at café > café owner buys his beer supply from *government supplier*.

Four independent small business owners benefit from this one CUC before it goes to the government. Small business is the backbone of the US economy, and can become the solid bedrock for a private Cuban economy. Ros-Lehtinen either has no grasp of this concept or she is blinded by her inbred hatred for Fidel Castro.

Here is an accounting of expenses for a humanitarian trip I took in February 2013:

Housing Casa particular six nights	120CUC
Meals (from private cafeterias/restaurants)	80CUC
Transp. 16 trips, including airport r/t	120CUC
Funds paid to private entrepreneurs	**320CUC**
Bottle rum, 4 bottles water, 1 bottle cola	10CUC
Crystal Beer 12 bottles	12CUC
Airport water and cookies	3CUC
Funds paid to the state	**25CUC**

So I paid 25 CUC to the Cuban state-operated stores. I invested 120 CUC in a couple and their three rambunctious young sons who loved the flannel pajamas I brought them. They put me in one of their casa particular rooms with a private bath, made my breakfast daily and gave me a fresh dry towel. They had me in comfort with air conditioning and hot and cold running water.

I invested a total of 120 CUC to an assortment of six different drivers. Each one was under age 35 and all had young families. One brought his 8-year-old son along as his co-pilot.

My meals came generally from a cafeteria: someone selling sandwiches, juices, and other items from a counter set up in their front door. I did have two meals at my favorite private restaurant La Rosa Negro. I can't resist their chicken cordon bleu for 4.95 CUC or their pina coladas for 1 CUC.

Multiply my investment in independent entrepreneurs by thousands of tourists and a new economy will take hold in Cuba. Entrepreneurs no longer would need the government and the government would be able to shed some of its bloated workforce.

Entrepreneurship is blooming in Cuba, yet it is hobbled by a lack of consumers and a lack of marketing, accounting, and business savvy. I have given guidance to several young entrepreneurs whose businesses are now doing well, but the majority of new Cuban entrepreneurs have no one to guide them. They are stuck behind a seawall, one not constructed by their government but by the US government.

Americans are adventurous and looking to help anywhere, especially young and idealistic students. Let them travel to Cuba. Let us set up mentoring programs where US college students could be paired with a small business owner. Spend a couple of month there – the owner would probably make room in their house for the student. There would be such great interaction that could lead to long term friendships and mentoring. But these Cuban entrepreneurs are stuck behind a seawall constructed by the US government.

It's time to tear down this seawall! Open the gates of tourism and work cooperatively with the Cuban government and universities to develop business training programs. Cuba has phenomenal universities dedicated to medicine, engineering, computer sciences, and the arts, but no real business school. Let American students and retirees go to Cuba and mentor new businesses, and watch entrepreneurship flourish.

Some in the Miami Cartel have argued that Cuba should give every employee (most people work for the state) a salary increase 10 times over or more. They suggest more government dependency! Isn't this what these same people rage about here in our country? The young people I have guided in start-up businesses want to grow their businesses, their income, and their lifestyle and never be dependent on the government again.

They love their country, they are proud of their country, and they want to see themselves and others prosper through their own talents. It's time to tear down that seawall and help make it a reality. Perhaps the spirit of Ronald Reagan could be summoned to stand across the Oval Office from President Obama and say, "Mr. Obama, tear down this seawall."

35. Blasts from the Past

No book about Cuba would be complete without a mention of the 1950s-era automobiles that play the streets of Cuba, mostly utilized as private taxis (entrepreneurship) due to their large seating capacity. And there aren't just a few of them – they are ubiquitous. They are well maintained by their owners and though replacement parts are unavailable from the US, it's not unusual to be walking down the street and seeing a car with its hood up and the owner working on it. He may have a grinding wheel or other implement on the sidewalk where he is fabricating a replacement part. Most 50's cars now have Toyota engines and power trains.

It would be very cool when the embargo is lifted if the Big 3 auto manufacturers would travel to Cuba with fleets of mini-vans and SUVs on cargo ships and trade them outright for the old Cuban cars. The cars could then be brought back to the US and sold to car aficionados to be restored.

Another diamond in the rough in Cuba is the number of antiques in the various homes. Many are quite stunning and have been in the families since before the Revolution. Staying in a casa particular can be an extraordinary event, especially for a lover of antiques who could see armoires, dressers, tables, chairs, and other furniture.

Bride and Groom and Videographer along the Malecon

36. Cuban Trivia

- Cubans answer the telephone with 'Dime' or 'Digeme' – 'Tell me'
- Cubans lack bathroom scales hence when women pass the bus station or are preparing to board a bus they go inside and weigh themselves on the luggage scale before God and country
- When Cubans are waiting to enter a public facility and you arrive you must determine who the last person before you to arrive was and then you are now the last one – they do not form lines
- When lining up inside a building, they will set their sandals in line and take a seat
- When a couple wants a divorce in Cuba there is no judicial process; they go to a notary who fills out the paperwork, they sign it, and they are divorced
- Cubans like to reverse first names within their family; some examples: Yanisley and Yelsinay; Reinaldo and Odlanier; Lizet and Tezil; Idania and Aidani; and my personal favorite, Boris and Sirob
- When you visit someone's home, the men all toast each other with a shot of ron (rum)

- The most romantic thing a Cuban can say to their lover is "Yo estoy muerta contigo." I am dead with you
- Cuban nurses still wear white uniforms and caps as did nurses in the US until the 1970s
- In dialing Cuban telephones, dialing a mobile phone requires a prefix of 5; landline a prefix of 7
- Cuban homes and commercial buildings all have concrete or ceramic floors; Cubans clean the floor by using a t-shaped long stick with a wet towel wrapped around the lower portion
- Colon Cemetery in Havana is a beautiful, historic cemetery going back to the early 20th century. Most of the tombs are marble and some have been vandalized through the years. When you attend a funeral or visit a grave as you drive out your car is stopped. Security guards check the truck to ensure you are not stealing marble
- Cubans come in three ethnic groups: Black, White, and Mulatta. When someone describes another, they mention their skin color while dragging two fingers across their left wrist, kind of like a baseball manager calling for a leftie reliever
- Cuban gyms have few real weights but that doesn't stop the workouts. I've seen everything you can imagine, including an engine block, and transmission gears made into a dumbbell
- When someone's day gets off to a good start in Cuba, they say 'I've painted the morning pink'
- When you see an address in Cuba printed or hand-written it looks like this:
  Oquendo, 455 % San Miguel y Belasquain
  Translated it means 455 Oquendo Street, Between San Miguel and Belasquain
- There are two inter-city bus lines in Cuba: Astra for Cubans and ViaZul for tourists. Fare between Havana and Santa Clara: Astra 1.5 CUC ViaZul 11.25 CUC. ViaZul operates beautiful air-conditioned motorcoaches with DVR video
- US Credit cards are not accepted in Cuba; it is an all cash excursion

- Jose Marti Airport in Havana has jet bridges with walls of tempered glass unlike the all steel bridges at US airport. They reflect heat rather than become a hot box, and they don't require lighting in the daytime –very energy efficient
- Cubana Airlines flight attendants wear reflective vests during take-off and landing so in the event of emergency passengers can identify them in the confusion
- Christmas in Cuba was banned in 1969, and reinstated in 1998. Where were Bill O'Reilly and FOX and Friends?
- Pedestrians do NOT have right-of-way in Cuba. Cars, trucks, and buses will bear down on you with horn blaring
- Cuba has good drinking water, and daily fresh baked bread in every corner of the country
- Since Internet service costs $70 per month, some people charge neighbors to have an email address on their computer
- The country's power grid is old, and they have roaming blackouts
- Cuban license plates denote a caste system: Yellow for the average person, usually older cars; Green for military, Blue for government, and Maroon for elite members of the Party – generally late model European or Japanese cars
- Cubans cannot afford home computers or laptops, so one of the most prized items in Cuba are flash drives; everybody has one to carry personal documents, pictures, etc. for use on work or university computers. The Miami Cartel spreads the myth that a person can be arrested for having a flash drive in their home. This is a fabrication repeatedly stated on MSNBC's Melissa Harris Perry Show in April 2013 by Mauricio Claver-Carone Executive Director of a Miami Cartel supported PAC in Washington, DC
- Many Cuban youths have x-Box and Play Station units and buy bootleg copies of games for fifty cents
- Notwithstanding the Embargo on the sale of US products to Cuba, the nightly news anchor in Cuba reads her news not from a TelePrompTer but from a Dell laptop with the Dell logo fully exposed

37. Personal Reflections

R eaders may wonder, what qualified me to write this book since I have no Cuban blood or affiliation. Well if you add up the number of days that half dozen or so Cuban-American members of the US House and Senate have spent in Cuba in the past 50 years, I outnumber their collective tally of zero. In a Congress where nothing happens internationally without a fact-finding trip how it that the Miami Cartel has managed to control and limit all interaction with one country without ever having visited?

When I set about to write this book it was originally going to be a sharing of the experiences I had with the Cuban people so that readers could get an idea of how kind, warm, and friendly they are. I have enjoyed a very unique privilege in Cuba. US diplomats are limited to a 25-mile radius of their offices, Congressional delegations spend their time with government officials, journalists are assigned escorts, and escorts also accompany the various People-to-People groups.

I have been able to travel unfettered across the country to numerous parishes. I have evangelized to and prayed the Rosary with hundreds of Catholics, some deep in their faith and some on the edge. My itinerary has always been fluid; move on or stick around based on the pulse of the parish. I would like to think that

I have come to know the people of Cuba, but I am certain of one thing: I have come to love them.

As I began to write I realized I had to connect the dots for the reader to help them understand how the whole Cuba debacle manifested itself, why things are the way that they are, and how much better they could be. I see the vile animosity the Miami Cartel harbors towards Fidel Castro and I get it, but I cannot get my arms around the whole anti-Christian and inhumane treatment of the 11 Million citizens of Cuba by the Miami Cartel.

I liken it to running a food bank and learning that one of your clients is abusing his wife and children. Now the Christian thing to do would be to continue to provide food to the wife and children. But in this case the 'Cuban Family' has been shut out altogether – for 54 years because of the perceived sins of the father!

As I researched and read comments from various US politicians I was left to wonder – do they hate Castro because of anything he has done, or simply because of who he is? Lord knows we have been cozy with many dictators over the past 50 years, the Shah of Iran and Saddam Hussein just to mention two. Why direct such hatred at Fidel and the people of his country? Considering that most Cuban-Floridians alive today were born in the US, why do they hate Castro and the people of Cuba? Cuba has never engaged in any hostility against them.

I truly believe in my heart that people within the Miami Cartel such as Ileana Ros-Lehtinen are truly evil. They glorify murder and revel in bringing misery to people's lives. Hence the driving force behind this book, to quote Edmund Burke is "All that is necessary for evil to triumph is for good men to do nothing." It's time the 11 Million Cubans had someone who spoke on their behalf.

To the Miami Cartel who continually whine about Castro and how they lost their property when they came to the US, I say, "Get over it! No one drove you out of Cuba – you left willingly. Some of you left early on to escape criminal prosecution for your roles in the Batista Dictatorship. It has been 54 years. Do you want to trade a comfortable, air-conditioned Florida bungalow for an un-air-conditioned cold water high rise in Havana? Probably not, so quit bellyaching!" I would ask the Cuban-Floridians: "Do you support reparations for African-Americans whose ancestors were brought here as slaves? No? Well you do not deserve any either."

We should immediately end the travel ban allowing Americans to travel to Cuba freely, and work towards unraveling the economic Blockade. In the military they talk about having *boots on the ground*. Well in Cuba I believe that what we need are *sneakers on the streets*. Imagine the country blanketed with thousands of Americans, especially young people who could connect with Cuba's young adults, sneakers on the streets.

That would be the ultimate People-to-People program. Stop pouring $40 Million a year down the Miami Cartel's Black Hole. That money could bring a better return if you gave $100 each to college students and told them to go help five families buy $20 worth of food. That's one month's pay for the average Cuban. The families might even be able to buy meat.

You could give $100 to 400,000 students. Even if some of them fleeced the money, the amount of direct aid provided to families in Cuba would be far greater than what the NGOs in the Miami Cartel's Black Hole provide. These 400,000 students would not need salaries, company cars, rents, telephony outlays, or engage in graft and supporting political campaigns financially, and they would be on their own for travel, not on the taxpayers' dime.

The Miami Cartel often makes claims about abuse of Cuban dissidents and their supporters. I have come to know several dissidents, and while there is some abuse still going on, it's not as widespread as the Miami Cartel would have us believe. They make it sound like North Korea. I saw people detained during the Pope's visit but they weren't dragged away in chains. The worst I have seen is the verbal and sometimes physical abuse of Los Damas de Blanco.

What if 100 Americans – some of the 'sneakers on the streets' armed with cameras were at St Rita's Church to observe a peaceful demonstration after mass by Las Damas de Blanco? Would there be any violence and abuse? It's likely not. Picture thousands of camera-toting American tourists from Pinar del Rio to Oriente documenting everyday life and activities and bonding with the Cuban people.

Eventually ending the Embargo/Blockade would result in jobs in both countries. There are thousands of buildings in Havana that need modernization and upgrading. The country needs building materials. Every sidewalk in Havana needs to be rebuilt. More raw materials will be needed. A new spirit of cooperation could be engendered based on American values, not on Miami Cartel retribution.

Fidel Castro made one attempt at cooperation in the recent past. In 2005 as the Hurricane Katrina debacle unfolded Fidel Castro reached out to the Bush administration offering to send a response team of 1,600 doctors to New Orleans. White House spokesman Scott McClellan did not acknowledge the offer; he just made some crass remark about Castro. I know many Cubans in the medical profession – doctors, nurses, therapists, and they are all well-educated and well experienced. They would have gladly helped citizens of the country that had abused them for 50 years.

Cooperation is what I prayed for when I was in Havana on Jan. 18, 2012 during a mission trip. Sitting in my apartment with a friend one evening we heard a loud rumble and felt the ground shake. It was not an earthquake it was a building nine blocks away collapsing.

We made our way there and I was on the pile in shorts and flip flops pulling away chunks of broken concrete. My friend was a doctor and she was setting up triage. Among the occupants of the building were a group of 10 high school students studying for an exam. I was relieved of my digging duties by military personnel who arrived. As I made my way back to the apartment I was praying, 'Let there please be an urban search and rescue team from Florida that is going to be here by sunrise with their search dogs.' And then I realized, oh wait this is Cuba; people in our government hate this country. I guess any souls under that rubble better pray that the people digging by hand get to them quickly. They deserved to be rescued but could not hope for any rescue efforts by the greatest country in the world.

38. Gratitude to the Catholic People of Cuba

Cuban families always have room for a guest to sleep. I've slept on double beds, single beds, sofas, cots, air mattresses that I've brought as gifts, and on blankets on the floor. I've shared sleeping accommodations with others. Although there are casa particulars across Cuba, when I visited a parish I sought the pastor's help to find accommodations. Rather than pay money to a 'rent room' owner I could give the host family assistance in procuring meat or chicken for their family.

My sincere gratitude to the people of the following parishes with whom I shared the Liturgy and who opened their hearts and homes to me:

- Iglesia de la Purisima Concepcion
- Iglesia de Nuestra Senora de la Merced
- Iglesia del Inmaculado Corazon de Maria
- Iglesia del Espiritu Santo
- Iglesia San Fransisco de Asis
- Iglesia Nuestra Senora de la Caridad del Cobre
- Iglesia Santa Croce in Gerusalemme
- Iglesia del Santo Cristo del Buen Viaje
- Iglesia Paroquia de Cardenas
- Iglesia Paroquia San Salvador de Bayamo

- Paroquia del Espiritu Santo
- Paroquia Iglesia de San Geronimo
- Paroquia Santo Angel Custodio
- Paroquia Nuestra Señora de la Candelaria
- Paroquia Nuestra Señora de Montserrat
- Paroquia del Espíritu Santo
- Catedral de San Eugenio de la Palma
- Catedral Santísimo Salvador de Bayamo
- Catedral de San. Isidore
- Catedral de San Carlos
- Catedral de San Rosendo
- Catedral of Santa Clara de Assisi
- Catedral de Nuestra Señora de la Asunción
- Catedral de la Virgen María de la Concepción Inmaculada (aka San Cristóbal)

I would like to acknowledge the following religious communities:

- Capuchin Fathers
- Sisters of the Sacred Heart
- Congregation of the Servants of Mary
- Congregation of the Servants of St. Joseph

I give a special acknowledgement to Jaime Lucas Cardinal Ortega y Alamino, Archbishop of San Cristobal de la Habana. He is a true man of God who has negotiated the release of almost 3,000 prisoners from Cuban jails and who is often attacked in the media by the Godless terrorist collaborators in the Miami Cartel.

And my deepest gratitude and prayers to my beloved Pastor and personal spiritual director, Padre Jaime of Nuestra Senora de la Caridad del Cobre for his continued ministry to the people of Habana Centro.

Mi amado pastor en La Habana, Padre Jaime

39. Small Gestures, Big Miracles

We can do no great things, only small things with great love. –
Mother Teresa

I am often asked by people if I think that as just one person I can
make a difference in and for Cuba. I'm reminded of the tale of
the young boy on a beach which is littered with hundreds of
starfish early in the morning. He is tossing them back into the sea
when an old man comes along and says, "Good morning, young
man! May I ask what it is you are doing?"

The boy responds, "Throwing these starfish back into the
ocean. The sun is coming up and the tide is going out. If I don't
throw them back in they'll die." The man says in reply, "Son,
there are hundreds of them here on this beach. You can't possibly
make a difference."

The boy smiles at the man and nods, then bends down and
picks up another starfish. He gives it a good toss and when it
lands on the water he says to the old man, "I made a difference
for that one." And as he walked along tossing starfish in the sea
he continued to call out, "And that one and that one..."

I coined my own saying in Cuba akin to Mother Teresa's
quote; *'The smaller the act, the bigger the miracle.'* I'd like to share
my four favorite miracles. A family I befriended lives in a small
house where the kitchen and living room combined measure
10' x 10.' They have no table but have four chairs along the wall

where they eat their meals with their plate in their lap, including an elderly grandmother.

On my subsequent trip I brought along a folding TV tray I purchased at Walmart. When mealtime came along I opened the box and set out the tray for Abuela, then put her plate on it. It was the first time she would eat off a table at home in 28 years and she cried. I headed west to Pinar del Rio with her adult grandson. When we returned several days later and were walking down the street people stepped out of their homes to acknowledge me. Abuela had invited the entire street in to see her miniature kitchen table!

When I was a patient at CIREN one evening I left the campus with other patients to walk to a local restaurant. As we returned and walked past the guard shack the guard called me over. "Are you the American?" After I replied he said, "I am taking an exam in two days on the English language. If I pass I can take a full English class. Would you sit with me until my shift ends at 6 a.m. and speak English with me?" I smiled and told him I would go to my patient house to use the rest room then come back.

I returned and told him that I had my daily meeting with my treatment team at 8 a.m. and then therapy so I couldn't possible stay up all night. Then I handed him my English-Spanish Dictionary. Tears welled in his eyes and he hugged me. Several days later he was at my patient house to return my dictionary and to tell me he'd passed the exam and was enrolled in the class. Several days later he brought his entire family to CIREN – wife, parents, and children to meet me and thank me!

One of the ways that Cubans can be supported by Americans is to put money into their mobile phone accounts via companies here in the US that offer special promotions: pay $20 and get $40 worth of minutes for a Cuban. One young man sent me the following email message: 'Last week when my grandmother die I was able to telephone my father in Mexico and other relative in Pinar del Rio and Camaguey because you put money in my telephone. If no telephone then mail letter take one week in Cuba two week get to Mexico. My heart is open large to thank you.

Next time you come Cuba you stay my house Mel sleep on sofa you sleep Mel bed and Juliet cook for you.' (SIC)

This last miracle I wish to cite was a cooperative effort with Attorney Bill Neal of Lewisville, Texas, and his wife Shelli. The Neals support my efforts and offered to donate 50 8GB flash drives to give to university students. When I arrived at the university and opened the box Bill had inadvertently given me a box containing 50 of his firm's presentation folders. I was upset and felt terrible to disappoint the students until they began to examine the folders. They'd never seen anything like them and asked if they could have them to present their thesis prior to graduation. They could make do with the smaller flash drives they currently had, but these folders would make them the envy of the university. They were thrilled.

So can one person make a difference in Cuba? Yes. By performing small acts that transcend into big miracles, a difference has been made in the lives of that grandmother, that guard, that grandson, those students, and for untold others. Bill Neal made a difference, and he never left a footprint in the country.

Epilogue

I. A Strategy for a Solution, Mr. President

I am no John Kerry, Henry Kissinger, or Colin Powell. I am no Madeline Albright, Hillary Clinton, or Condoleezza Rice.

What I am is a Roman Catholic who is tired of seeing the 54-year hate fest perpetuated by the Miami Cartel against the innocent people of Cuba. I am a student of world history and current events, and someone who spent the last 20 years of his career as a sales performance consultant, teaching selling and negotiating skills.

I understand how during negotiations to evaluate an opponent's position, how to leverage one's position, and most importantly how to lead the negotiation to a conclusion whereby the sides are no longer opponents but collaborators and allies.

Mr. President, what the Cuban government wants, and what every man, woman, and child in Cuba wants is the return home of the Five Heroes, the Cuban Five. These individuals were convicted in a South Florida state of mass hysteria. No crimes were committed against the US, nor against any individual. Not one drop of blood was shed as a result of their actions.

There is nothing morally wrong with returning them to their families; it is in fact the moral thing to do. The only blow-back would come from South Florida. Mr. President, you are a much more compassionate and Christian person than the Miami Cartel.

The first concession we would want would be the return of Alan Gross who was convicted of equally dubious charges. President Raul Castro is ready for this exchange as he told Vatican Secretary of State Cardinal Bertone back in 2008.

In addition you could put these conditions on the table for consideration, Mr. President:

- Release from Cuban prisons of all relatives of Las Damas de Blanco – and they be guaranteed passports if they want to travel away from Cuba
- That you Mr. President address the Cuban people by television, announcing the return of the Cuban Five and announcing a new era of relations between the US and Cuba
- That Cuba expand accessibility to the Internet and cellular service via reduced costs by ETECSA or competition from US companies, and by expanding utilization of the undersea Internet cable from Venezuela to increase speed and bandwidth
- Reduce the cost by ETECSA of telephone calls to the US
- Grant Cubans access to Twitter which their government leaders enjoy
- Grant Cubans access to Skype to better communicate with family in the US and elsewhere
- Grant access to Cuba for FedEx and/or UPS to serve the island (bilaterally)
- Agree to lift the travel ban to allow open travel by tourists to Cuba if all the agreed upon stipulations are met within six months Agree to drop the state sponsor of terrorism designation
- If a mutual agreement is reached, arrange for an exchange of the Cuban Five and Alan Gross in Cancun, Mexico

Mr. President, whether it has been celebrities or members of Congress weighing in on either side's prisoners they have asked for a unilateral release. Please Mr. President it's time to employ diplomacy that will not only improve many lives but will also put our countries on a more solid footing. This could be the greatest legacy of your presidency. And Mr. President I offer my time and service to assist in any way those who may become involved in negotiations.

II. Dear President Obama

Pleas to President Barack Obama from ordinary Cubans from across Cuba. (Translated and modified only where necessary for clarity)

1.

Mr. President,

When I was born, 40 years ago, on this island called Cuba, the Cold War was front page of every newspaper, your country and mine were on different sides with totally opposite ideologies. Nuclear espionage, sabotage, communism, capitalism wild Russians and Americans were the words that topped all predecessors discussions. Our economic survival was the reason for the alliance with Union Sovietica. That decision was made in and whether it was correct or not, whether it was a smart move or not is irrelevant at this point.

Years have passed and all that Cold War is in the past, the stronger power made stronger but did not change its relationship with my country. Higher walls fell that divided the country but not on the island where the island I was born. Was left alone in the middle of the sea, seized economically without reason and having to turn to Venezuela and Chine for assistance. The Cuban people are very peaceful, sociable, hardworking and do not understand why we can not trade and exchange with a country so close to us. I am a married man I have three children over 40 years of life. When one of my children ask me why you keep I really cannot tell. My youngest son is a genius about baseball. I dream of take him to Yankee Stadium some day before I die.

Mr. President, you have in your hands the ability to make history and open all doors and sterilize absurd prohibitions that still remain between our countries. Please show the world your love of democracy and respect for the opinion of others and self-determination of peoples. Mr. President that his people deserve to smoke a good cigar or a drink a good taste of rum and we want refresh ourselves with a Coca Cola or eat a hot dog or at McDonald on our Malecon.

Sincerely,
PHT

2.

Dear Presidente Obama,

I know the American people were very sad when Pan Americano flight 103 was exploded over the sky in the England. And also very sad on the 11 septiembre when the airplanes crash in the Twin Towers. All Cubans were sad for America. In both determinations the people who committed these crimes faced justice.

The Cuban people have suffered too. On 6 octubre 1976 Cubana flight 455 was exploded from the sky. Many young people were killed including my family member. The terrorist who exploded the plane lives freely in your Miami. He is protected by the Miami Mafia and Ileana Ros and the goubernor Jed Bush brother of the Presidente Bush. Mister Presidente Obama I ask on behalf of all Cubans that you not allow this circus to go on. Luis Posada should be brought to Cuba for answer this criminal act and bombings in Havana at La Bodegita del Media that kill one person.

Please Mr. Presidente do what God believes should be done and do not let Posada go to his tomb with a laugh on his face.

Sincerely,
MLT

3.

Dear Mr. President,

The United States has a very good man in Paulo Lebon who come here and teach me how to begin my business. Paul is modest man and does not like praise. He say all the time that I am just

American acting like American do. If there are million more like Paulo please stop the Bloqueo and let them come to Cuba and help many more of us.

When I work for the state I get paid 24 CUC a month. Now with my business I made over 100 CUC a month. My wife and babies thank very much Paulo for his help me with business. Please stop the Bloqueo so many more kind Americans come help the Cuban people. I thank you for taking the time to read my letter and I wish all good to you and your bonita wife and daughters.

Sincerely,
NRH

4.

Dear Mr. President Obama,

We in Cuba are very wonderful people. We love our leader Fidel Castro. And that is our choice to believe. Our country has never done any bad to your country. Bad people in your country have done bad things to our Cuba. Grateful we are for you lift limitations money transfers so family in USA send to us. Please I beg you take more step to improve for us our life in Cuba by kill the Bloqueo. You will become a hero in my country and we would welcome you with open hearts and speech at Place de la Revolucion. God Bless Cuba and America and her peoples.

Sincerely,
YNC

5.

Dear President Obama,

You are a man who loves the beautiful beach with his family in Hawaii. I see on television. Have you ever see Varadero Beach in Cuba? Very pretty with sand beautiful and water very blue. No crowd like beach in Cancun or Hawaii. Please to come with your family and enjoy our sunshine our sand and our ron. You have mojito or Cuba libre or cerveza. Then you see how beautiful our Varadero and how friendly Cuban people. Maybe then you think about end Bloqueo. Thank you for the honor of read my letter.

Sincerely,

YAG

6.

Mr. President good day sir!

I drive LADA car very old and many times not work and have to fix myself with my brother. On television see cars in USA very nice would like to buy. I work as driver and when car not work I no work. With American car I make much money buy house for me and my wife and three children no longer live with my grandparent.

Please Mr. President it time has come to be for end of Bloqueo. You born 1961 and Bloqueo born 1958. As black man you bring change to USA as first black man president. Please bring change to Cuba with Bloqueo end.

Sincerely,

LYP

7.

Dear Presidente Obama,

In this moment I wish to inform you about what our Jefe Fidel Castro has meant to me. Like you I am a black man. I was born in 1950 so my child years were the Batista years. Black people were trash. We were called nigger even young children. When the Revolucion was a success Fidel opened all schools to blacks. My older brothers never shared a school with white children. I did all my life including the opportunity given to me by Fidel Castro to attend university. He was like your Martin Luther King. He is a good man and is very old. Please do not make us wait until he is dead to end the Bloqueo like Ileana Ros and the Diaz-Balarts want to happen. Let Fidel be part of the end of the Bloqueo. Thank you for your attention and God Bless you.

Sincerely,

OHM

8.

Dear President Obama,

This year Cuban government stopped the restrictions to travel and no longer need exit visa. Cubans may travel anywhere in the world free except United States. Because President Bush said we have terrorists in Cuba we cannot travel freely to US. To take visa application at embassy wait two years for appointment. Why so long Mr. President? My friend Paulo LeBon say me that if no more list of terror country then go to US no problem. I would like to visit US and come to Washington see many statues of many great men and go Mount Rushmore more great men. If we are welcome to USA we will welcome America people to Cuba anytime.

Sincerely,

LHO

9.

Mr. President Obama,

I listen to news on television about USA and I hear many people not work. I am not certain how it all works but I think if Cuba buy many things from USA then more people work in USA. Cuba buy very much from China far far away take much time for boats to come to Cuba. Boat from Miami to Cuba arrive 12 hours. Stores not empty so long if product come from Miami.

Please ask you Mr President finish the bloqueo and let Cubans buy good quality from USA. China quality not so good. Box fall apart. Thank you my friend.

Sincerely,

RAD

10.

Dear President Obama,

Salute to you sir. I want to tell you about my country because I think you never visit here. Cuba is very beautiful country. People

warm people friendly people simpatico. Welcome tourist from Canada whose airplane fly over United States. Welcome tourist from Europa. Want to welcome tourist from USA and make friend with them. It is 150 kilometer from La Habana to Florida Key West. If we had long arms we could touch hands across the ocean. For now we wait for the airplane from USA to bring tourists to become our new friends. Mr. President please finish the Bloqueo.
Sincerely,
VDR

11.

Dear Mr. President,
My grandparents lived under Fulgencio Batista. They died now but always talk about evil of Batista and Ministry of Interior. Fidel Castro make life better for all Cubans but America punish Cuba. Never understand because Cuba not do any bad to USA. But people in Miami do much bad to Cuba kill many people not military on airplanes and in street. Mr. President I plead you please end embargo and punish of Cuban people.
Sincerely,
GLC

12.

Dear President Obama,
I know that you are a Christian man I share with you what I learn in Bible school: You shall love your neighbor as yourself - Mateo 22:39
Please love the people of Cuba.
Sincerely,
MEL

Appendix A

The following is a list of terrorist acts perpetrated on US soil by US-based anti-Castro groups from the period 1967 - 1975[64]

1967 April 3. New York City–The Cuban Mission to the United Nations is bombed; U.N. acting chief suffers non-fatal burns in the bombing

October 16. New York City–There are explosions across from the Cuban, Yugoslav, and Finnish missions to the United Nations

1968 January 25. Miami, Fla– Package en route to Cuba explodes; El Poder Cubano is suspected

February 8. –Miami, Fla.–The British consulate is damaged by a bomb. El Poder Cubano or other anti-Castro Cubans are believed responsible

April 18. New York City–The Mexican mission to the US is bombed by El Poder Cubano, an anti-Castro group

May 26. Miami Fla.–The Mexican consul general's residence is damaged by a bomb placed by El Poder Cubano

June 21. New York City–Spanish Nationalist Tourist office is again bombed by El Poder Cubano

July 4. New York City–The Canadian consulate and the tourist office are bombed by El Poder Cubano. The

64   cuban-exile.com/doc_176-200/doc0180.html

Australian National Tourist Office is bombed by El Poder Cubano

July 7. New York City–The Japanese National Tourist Office is bombed by El Poder Cubano

July 9. New York City–The Yugoslav and Cuban missions to the United States are bombed by El Poder Cubano

July 14. Chicago, Ill.–El Poder Cubano terrorists bomb the Mexican National Tourist Office

July 16. Newark, N.J.–A bomb planted by El Poder Cubano is found and removed from the Mexican consulate by police

July 19. Los Angeles, Calif.–An Air France ticket office is damaged by a bomb

A Mexican National Tourist Office is bombed

A Shell Oil building is bombed   .

A Japan Air Lines office is bombed

El Poder Cubano is suspected of all the bombings

July 30. Los Angeles, Calif.–Anti-Castro Cuban terrorists bomb the British consulate

August 3. New York City–The Bank of Tokyo Trust Company is bombed by El Poder Cubano

August 5. Los Angeles, Calif.–The British consulate is bombed by anti-Castro Cubans

August 8. Miami, Fla.–An underwater explosion by El Poder Cubano damages a British vessel near Miami.

Los Angeles, Calif.–The British consulate is bombed; the bombing is claimed by anti-Castro Cuban exiles

August 17. Miami, Fla.,–A Mexican airline office is bombed by El Poder Cubano

September 16. Miami, Fla.–El Poder Cubano terrorists fire on a Polish vessel with rifles

June 8. New York City–A bomb explodes in Loew's Orpheum Theater, causing minor damage; press reports alleged that it was set by anti-Castro Cubans protesting a showing of the picture 'Che'

1970 May 5. Coral Gables, Fla.–The University of Miami Computer Center is firebombed

1972 March. Sometime in March, the Secret Cuban Government bombs a theater in New York and two drug stores in San Juan, P.R.

March 29. Biscayne, Fla.–A Soviet research ship is bombed by JCN, an anti-Castro Cuban group it is suspected that JCN was used as a cover name

June 14. San Juan, P.R.–A liquor store is bombed by Anti-Communist Commandos (possibly an alias used by FLNC, Cuban National Liberation Front)

December. Sometime in December–A travel agency in Queens, N.Y., is bombed; the incident is attributed to FIN, an anti-Castro group

December 11. New York City–The VA-Cuba Forwarding Company is bombed by FIN, an anti-Castro group

1973 March 28. New York City–The Center for the Cuban Studies is bombed; it is claimed by Secret Cuban Government

March 29. Union, N.J.–There is an attempt (possibly by FIN, Cuban National Front) to bomb a bookstore

July 24. New York City–The Martin Luther King, Jr., Labor Center is bombed; it is claimed by Secret Cuban Government; a pro-Castro Cuban exhibition is being held in the building

December. Month of December–A business office in the New York City area is bombed by the Secret Cuban Government

Miami, Fla.–A Bahamian cargo ship is bombed by the FLNC (using the Cuban Anti-Communist League as an alias)

December 30. Miami, Fla.–A British freighter is bombed; it is attributed to the Cuban Action or FIN (National Integration Front)

1974 April 13. Miami, Fla.–Jose de la Torriente, former Cuban minister of agriculture, is killed by a sniper; Zero, anti-Castro group of Cuban exiles, takes responsibility

November 9. Washington, D.C.–A bombing of the Organization of American States building is claimed by

FLNC (using Cuban Movement C-4 as an alias), an anti-Castro group.

1975 February 1. New York City.–The Venezuelan Consulate is bombed by Abdala, an anti-Castro student group

February 6. Los Angeles, Calif.– Unidos, a socialist book-store run by the October League, is bombed; the Cuban Action Commandos are suspected

February 26. Los Angeles, Calif.–KCET, a radio station, is bombed; the Cuban action Commandos are suspected because the station had just announced the showing of a Cuban film, 'Lucia'

March 27. Los Angeles, Calif.–Two buildings, one housing the Panama Government Tourist Bureau and the other housing the Costa Rican Consulate, are damaged slightly by separate bomb blasts; the Cuban Action Commandos (an anti-Castro group) are suspected; Panama and Costa Rica had supported Cuba's readmission to the Organization of American States

April 3. Los Angeles, Calif.–An attempted bombing of the Communist Party office misfires; the Cuban Action Commandos are suspected

April 13. Los Angeles, Calif.–A bomb is dropped through the roof of the Unidos book store; the store has a left-wing orientation; the Cuban Action Commandos claim credit through a caller

May 2. Santa Monica, Calif.–A Socialist Workers Party bookstore is bombed by the CAC (Cuban Action Commandos)

May 7. Los Angeles, Calif.–The leftist-oriented Midnight Special Bookstore is bombed; the Cuban Action Commandos are suspected

June 17. Elizabeth, N.J.–More than 100 Cuban-Americans are arrested after resentment against police culminates in a traffic-blocking protest and stone throwing near police headquarters

July 15. Los Angeles, Calif.–The Mexican consulate is bombed; four people are injured; $35,000 damage is done; it is suspected that the bombing was a joint action of the Hungarian Peace and Freedom Fighters, the Cuban Action Commandos, and the Nazi Group

July 18. Washington, D.C.–A bomb placed outside the Costa Rican embassy does not completely detonate; although Cuban Scorpion claims credit, statements from an FLNC leader implicate Abdala and the Cuban Action Commandos

October 6. Miami, Fla.–The Dominican Republic consulate is bombed; the bombing is attributed to FINC-Youth of the Stars

October 10. Ft. Lauderdale, Fla.–The Broward County courthouse is bombed; the bombing is attributed to FLNC, an anti-Castro group

October 17. Miami, Fla.–A bomb explodes in a luggage locker at Miami International Airport; it might have been aimed at a Dominican Airlines ticket counter

November 27. Miami, Fla.–A time bomb in the restroom of a Bahamas Airlines jet is set to go off as passengers are loading for Nassau; a call indicates the bombing is anti-Castro and that a group called Cuban Power '76 is responsible

December 3. Miami, Fla.–Identical bombs explode on the eve of a visit by William D. Rogers, US Secretary of State for Inter-American Affairs, at the Social Security building, the Florida State Employment Service office, two Post Office buildings, and the FBI headquarters building

December 4. Miami, Fla.–The Miami police department and Metropolitan Justice building are bombed; and anti-Castro group, JIN, claims responsibility; this is unique because the attack is against government buildings; usually these attacks are against businesses dealing with Cuba; an extortion note in Spanish demands $50 Million to be given to poor or the bombings would continue; the note is signed 'El Condor'

Appendix A

The following is a list of terrorist acts perpetrated on US soil by any Castro-supported interests from the period 1967 - 1975

(None Perpetrated)

Final Score

Cuban-American Terrorists Against US	Cuban-Backed Interests
63	0

And who according to the Miami Cartel are the evil ones?

Appendix B

Complete transcript of testimony before US Senate Subcommittee on May 3, 1960 by Rafael Lincoln Diaz Balart.

Communist Threat to the United States Through the Caribbean
U.S. Senate Subcommittee to Investigate the Administration of the Internal Security Act and Other Internal Security Laws, of the Committee on the Judiciary.

Tuesday, May 3, 1960[65]

Testimony of Rafael Lincoln Diaz Balart

AFTERNOON SESSION

The subcommittee reconvened at 2:15 p.m., pursuant to recess.
(Present: Senators Dodd and Keating; Mr. Sourwine and Mr. Mandel.)
Senator DODD. Please come to order.
Because we have a witness who wishes to leave the city today, we will interrupt the testimony of Father Perez, with Father Perez' permission, and call instead Mr. Diaz Balart.

---

65 latinamericanstudies.org/us-cuba/diaz-balart.htm

Representative ANFUSO. Mr. Chairman, Senator Keating, it is my very happy privilege this afternoon to introduce to this committee Dr. Rafael Diaz Balart, a former Senator of Cuba, a man who studied for many years in this country, who is a devoted citizen of his country, a disciple of the famous hero of Cuba, Marti. He has been a resident of the United States, which country he has always worshiped because of its democratic principles, and it has always been his idea to carry out those principles in his native land.

He knows a great deal about the present difficulties going on in Cuba today. He feels deeply that the country is going communistic, that it is being alienated from the United States, for which the people of Cuba have always had a great love and admiration. He feels deeply that the people of Cuba do not like the separation which their dictator form of government is leading them to. He happens to be a brother-in-law of the present ruler of Cuba, not by choice, but it is something that happened.

And he is here, I am sure, to tell this committee the whole truth about Cuba. And I can assure the committee that he will be very cooperative, as he has been in the past with the staff of this committee, and is indeed at your disposal. I thank you very much for this opportunity of being able to present him.

Senator DODD. Raise your right hand, please.

Do you solemnly swear the testimony you will give before this subcommittee will be the truth, the whole truth, and nothing but the truth, so help you God?

Mr. DIAZ BALART. I do.

Senator DODD. Have a chair. You speak English, I believe.

Mr. DIAZ BALART. Yes, sir, a little bit.

Senator DODD. If you need an interpreter, she will be present.

Mr. DIAZ BALART. Thank you.

Mr. SOURWINE. Your full name, sir?

Mr. DIAZ BALART. Rafael Lincoln Diaz Balart.

Mr. SOURWINE. And your residence?

Mr. DIAZ BALART. I live in New York.

Mr. SOURWINE. You are a lawyer?

Mr. DIAZ BALART. Yes, sir.

Mr. SOURWINE. Are you a member of the bar of Cuba?

Mr. DIAZ BALART. Yes, Sir.

Mr. SOURWINE. Are you a member of the bar of any State of the United States?

Mr. DIAZ BALART. No, Sir.

Mr. SOURWINE. Where did you go to school?

Mr. DIAZ BALART. Havana, University, and University of Oriente.

Mr. SOURWINE. When?

Mr. DIAZ BALART. From 1945, when I started Havana University.

Mr. SOURWINE. Did you have a prominent classmate in law school?

Mr. DIAZ BALART. Yes. I was a classmate of Premier Castro.

Mr. SOURWINE. You were a classmate of Fidel Castro?

Mr. DIAZ BALART. Yes.

Mr. SOURWINE. Were you formerly a member of the National Legislature of Cuba?

Mr. DIAZ BALART. Yes, Sir.

Mr. SOURWINE. How long have you been in the United States?

Mr. DIAZ BALART. Since January 15, 1959.

Mr. SOURWINE. Why did you leave Cuba and come here?

Mr. DIAZ BALART. I left Cuba, on December 20, 1958, to Europe, for some professional business, find while there the Communist forces of Castro arrived to power, so I remained there until January 15 when I came here, to the United States.

Senator KEATING. May I inquire? You mean that your relationship is that your wife is a sister of Fidel Castro?

Mr. DIAZ BALART. No my sister was the wife of Castro.

Senator KEATING. I See. Thank you.

Mr. DIAZ BALART. I would like to ask Your Honor's permission to read a very brief opening statement, if it is possible.

Senator DODD. All right. Go ahead.

Mr. DIAZ BALART. As a Cuban, and as a public person, I appreciate the hospitality extended to me by this great brother country of the United States of America. I am happy to respond to the subpoena of this distinguished committee to appear before it. I do so with the same feeling of appreciation as I would if I were invited to come before any other representative body of the, other free countries of America in order to cooperate with my best knowledge towards the understanding of our mutual problems, and for the better defense of the democratic Christian principles that are fundamental in the Americas. These principles are increasingly being threatened from Alaska to the Rio Plata, by the subversive activities of imperialistic and atheistic international Communists. Fulfilling this appearance, which I have been requested to do by this honorable committee, I wish to emphasize my profound faith in the moral resources of the Cuban people.

I am sure that they know how to proceed in the struggle for the total liberation from Communist tyranny and oppression that today is ruling that country, and from their spreading hatred and provocation throughout the Western Hemisphere.

I wish also to give this committee and public opinion generally a clear and definite assurance of my devotion to the friendship and solidarity of the peoples of the American Continent. And I want to express my respect and faith in the principle of nonintervention in the internal affairs of the respective countries, which are fundamental principles of the Organization of the American States.

I shall always have profound love for this great country of liberty and brotherhood. Thank you very much.

Senator DODD. All right, Sir. Thank you.

Go ahead, Mr. Sourwine.

Senator KEATING. Just one question. You are a citizen of Cuba?

Mr. DIAZ BALART. Yes, Sir.

Senator KEATING. Thank you.

Mr. SOURWINE. Congressman Anfuso mentioned that you were Fidel Castro's brother-in-law, and you said that your sister was Fidel Castro's wife. I take it your use of the past tense means that she no longer is his wife.

Mr. DIAZ BALART. That is right.

Mr. SOURWINE. Is your sister still alive?

Mr. DIAZ BALART. Yes, Sir.

Mr. SOURWINE. She is then divorced from Fidel Castro?

Mr. DIAZ BALART. That is right.

Senator KEATING. Is she living in Cuba?

Mr. DIAZ BALART. Yes.

Mr. SOURWINE. Mr. Diaz Balart, did you ever hold a position in the Government of Cuba?

Mr. DIAZ BALART. Yes, Sir.

Mr. SOURWINE. What position?

Mr. DIAZ BALART. I was Under Secretary of Interior, before being elected a congressman.

Mr. SOURWINE. When was that?

Mr. DIAZ BALART. 1952.

Mr. SOURWINE. Under Batista?

Mr. DIAZ BALART. Yes, Sir.

Mr. SOURWINE. Did you ever hold office under any President other than Batista?

Mr. DIAZ BALART. No, Sir.

Mr. SOURWINE. Were you, then, a pro-Batista Cuban? You were part of the Batista government?

Mr. DIAZ BALART. Yes. I was pro-Batista before 1952, when the party that he founded-he called it a new party, and he called the Cuban youth to join that party in order to fight for order, for progress, and for stability of the Cuban country. And I liked those principles. I joined him in the opposition. I was the leader of the youth party in all the nation while we were in the opposition. And in 1952, when the coup d'état took place-in 1952, 10th of March-I continued with Batista, because he promised to give the country progress and stability, and I was very much concerned with the terrible situation of my country before those years when the life, the human life didn't have any value at all. And being a Christian, as I am, I have always thought that it is not possible to think in any other human principle in any country if you don't have before anything the guarantee of the human life, and of the human dignity.

Mr. SOURWINE. When did you leave the Batista government?

Mr. DIAZ BALART. I was elected in 1954 a congressman, and I continued within the government of Batista with very definite and peculiar point of view, as head of the youth movement. We were asking Batista in private and in public for honesty in the government, for progress, for stability, for free elections, and there is a matter of record, even in the U.S. magazine like Time, of that time, when we asked in a big rally of more than 80,000 young men and women all throughout the island headed by me, we asked Batista to have free elections.

Mr. SOURWINE. Did you ever break with Batista?

Mr. DIAZ BALART. I had a lot of struggle with Batista, and that is also a matter of record in all the press of my country. After I was elected in 1954, as the No. 1 of all the representatives of my province, I denounced the corruption of those elections in my Oriente Province, and I had trouble with Batista. After the big rally in 1953, I made very clear in my speech before the Presidential Palace, that we didn't agree with the politics of Batista, that we didn't agree with the cabinet of Batista, and because of that I was out of the country for several months.

Mr. SOURWINE. Did you return?

Mr. DIAZ BALART. I returned, and I had a meeting with my organization, national organization, several times. We were making pressure in the government of Batista for progress. We were asking for a land reform, a constitutional land reform, and we were expecting to make Batista to have some changes. After that, when the civil war was working, and working in spite of our efforts when Castro led the attack to the Moncada barracks in 1953, before that there was not a single death in the situation of Cuba. Castro provoked it, without any reason in that moment – the attack on the Moncada barracks, with 80 men, knowing, as you can realize very easily, that he was not going to fulfill. And besides that, that he had any chances to get the barracks, he was not able to do anything with that. Then he just made that attack in order to promote himself as a leader in his own party.

After that a civil war started. And we realized it, in meetings one after another, in my organization, that then Fidel Castro, with the backing of the international machinery of the Communists, was going to get the power if other sectors of the Cuban public life was fighting openly against the Batista regime. So we had to choose between maybe two evils at that moment, and we knew what it would mean to our country that Fidel Castro and he Communists would get power.

That was the whole story of my attitude in that time.

Mr. SOURWINE. You never supported Fidel Castro, then?

Mr. DIAZ BALART. Not at all. I attacked him.

Mr. SOURWINE. You never supported the 26th of July Movement?

Mr. DIAZ BALART. No; I denounced in the very beginning, in the press of my country, when Raul Castro, which I know very well personally, since he, started to study the Communist doctrine, and he started to be a Communist agent – I denounced that in the press of my country, though I was in that moment a friend in a personal affair, and I told the public opinion of my country the danger of believing in the Castro Movement, not only because they were above all Communists, but also because I knew very well, as the public opinion of Cuba knew, that Castro was nothing else than an opportunist and a gangster, that had started his public life as a juvenile delinquent. And that is a matter of record in the press of Cuba, also.

Mr. SOURWINE. We have a great many witnesses to hear, Mr. Diaz Balart, and I don't want to cut you off at all, but I should like to request, with the permission of the Chair, that you keep your answers to the questions as short as you can. If you think you are being cut off when you have information you want to give, just tell us.

Mr. DIAZ BALART. Thank you very much.

Senator DODD. Before you leave this question, I do not think it is clear on the record – you opposed and criticized Batista at times, and you opposed Castro. And you made the remark, "I left the country for a few months." What year?

Mr. DIAZ BALART. That was 1953, November.

Senator DODD. When did you return?

Mr. DIAZ BALART. I returned 2 months after.

Senator DODD. Two months?

Mr. DIAZ BALART. Three months after.

Senator DODD. In 1953?

Mr. DIAZ BALART. That is right.

Senator DODD. And you were in Cuba continuously from 1953 until when?

Mr. DIAZ BALART. Until December 20, 1958.

Senator DODD. Then you went to Europe?

Mr. DIAZ BALART. Yes, sir.

Senator DODD. Then you came to the United States from Europe?

Mr. DIAZ BALART. That is correct.

Senator KEATING. May I ask one other question? When you say you left the country, was that because Batista ordered you to leave?

Mr. DIAZ BALART. No, not exactly, no. I was a member of the Government, but within the Government I led the youth movement. We had a struggle within the Government, so I felt that it was better to–

Senator DODD. Was it because of Batista or not?

Mr. DIAZ BALART. No; I cannot say that.

Senator DODD. You left on your own?

Senator KEATING. Did you leave under any pressure?

Mr. DIAZ BALART. No, not at all. It was moral pressure, because I–

Senator KEATING. Any threats?

Mr. DIAZ BALART. No, not at all. No threats. It was a question of moral and ideological point of view.

Mr. SOURWINE. The youth movement you speak of would be called in English the Youth of Action Progressive Party?

Mr. DIAZ BALART. Yes, it was a Youth of Action Unitarian Party when we were in the opposition, and Action Progressive Party when we were in the Government.

Mr. SOURWINE. Now, you were opposed to Castro. Were you also opposed to Prio?

Mr. DIAZ BALART. Yes, I was opposed to Prio when Prio was in power.

Senator KEATING. You were opposed to all these people?

Mr. DIAZ BALART. Yes.

Senator KEATING. Who were you for?

Mr. DIAZ BALART. I am for the liberty and progress of my country.

Senator KEATING. I mean you didn't have any particular individual?

Mr. DIAZ BALART. No. In that time, I was in favor of Batista, because I thought, before 1952, that he was a solution for the Cuban people. He had left the power in 1944, after 11 years being in power, and having all the power in his hands – he lost an election, a general election, and he left the power, he gave to his worst enemy the power, and he visit all the countries of Latin America as a democratic hero. So he was a real hope for the Cuban people – at least I thought that that was the situation.

Senator KEATING. But you became disillusioned about Batista in what year?

Mr. DIAZ BALART. Increasingly. I personally continued being his friend, but increasingly I talked to him, and I told him publicly also that he should give progress and another attitude to his government.

Senator KEATING. Would it be fair to say that you were anti-Batista when you left to go to Europe?

Mr. DIAZ BALART. Pardon me, Sir?

Senator KEATING. Were you anti-Batista, against Batista, when you left to go to Europe?

Mr. DIAZ BALART. Ideologically, yes. But I cannot say politically I was yet against Batista, because, we were in a civil war, and I thought, and my movement thought, that to oppose publicly and definitely to Batista would mean in that moment to help the Castro movement, which had the weapons and had all the sources to get power. And we knew that as soon as the power was out of the hands of Batista, by a violent means, not by a normal means, as we were expecting to be, we knew that the only one that was going to get the power was Fidel Castro, and the Communists. Not even Carlos Prio or any of the other people.

Senator KEATING. Now, let me ask you this. Do you consider the Castro dictatorship worse than the Batista dictatorship?

Mr. DIAZ BALART. It is very different. The Batista dictatorship was only a political dictatorship. The Castro dictatorship can only be compared in America, I think, to Peron, and even much worse than Peron, because the Castro dictatorship is a complete and a, total dictatorship. I think that is the first real example of absolute and complete totalitarian government in the American Hemisphere. And, besides that, and above all, is the first real Communist state in our hemisphere.

Senator KEATING. You consider it a Communist state?

Mr. DIAZ BALART. Absolutely. I don't think there is any doubt in this moment in the minds of any that is a student of the Communist tactics and the Communist struggle. The point is that, as I have told several times – for instance, when they asked me is Castro a Communist, I remember a professor that I had in the law school, that always taught also when you are going to talk about a very important matter you should start sharpening the terminology, and it is important when somebody asks if Castro or is anybody a Communist, it is important to know what do they mean by Communist.

Now, Castro is not a card holder of the Communist Party in Cuba, never has been. But, at the same time, the card holder of the Socialistic Party, or the Communist Party in Cuba, maybe a lot of them are less dangerous and less important members of the Communist machinery.

What happens is that Castro is a member of the Third International, which they don't, have a card never.

I want to affirm, with all my faith and all my knowledge, that Fidel Castro is the most important and most dangerous member in the Western Hemisphere of the Communist International machinery since the Russian revolution.

Senator KEATING. You don't favor the return of Batista, do you?

Mr. DIAZ BALART. We are very, very much opposed to that. We formed a movement, an underground movement, which is working very hard in Cuba, with two principal purposes – to overthrow the dictatorship of the Communists, and to prevent any possibility of the return to power of Batista.

Mr. SOURWINE. Is that organization the so-called Blanco Rosa, the White Rose?

Mr. DIAZ BALART. Yes, Sir.

Mr. SOURWINE. Do you hold a position in that organization?

Mr. DIAZ BALART. Yes, Sir; I am the founder and the general secretary.

Senator DODD. Let me ask you a question. You said you thought Castro succeeded because he overthrew Batista. Was there any third place you could have looked for some decent element to control the Government of Cuba?

Mr. DIAZ BALART. That is a very nice question. In that moment, Sir, with the civil war extended, we tried to have that third position, or third possibility, several times.

Senator DODD. Did you have a man who you thought would make a good president of Cuba?

Mr. DIAZ BALART. Not personally I, but there was the possibility. There was, for instance, Dr. Marquez Sterling, who was a candidate of the opposition in the election. But what happened is that Fidel Castro had all the weapons, all the backing of the Communist machinery – money, weapons, propaganda, and at the same time, because of the very intelligent propaganda of the Communist International machinery, he got the help of the right men, and of the right personality – even of the organization of the founder's rights. So Fidel Castro had at this moment, because of the very intelligent Communist propaganda, he had the help, the decisive help of the Communists and of the enemies of the Communists. So in that moment practically to anybody that studied the Cuban situation, in the middle of the civil war, there was not any other possibility, and the history, the recent history, has proved that we had.

Senator DODD. Did you ever suggest to Batista he withdraw in favor of a moderate candidate?

Mr. DIAZ BALART. We suggested to him to give free elections. We suggested to him in 1956 that – after the amnesty that favored Fidel Castro himself – we suggested a partial election of all the House of Representatives, all the Senate, and Governors, In order to have the basis, in order to have a change

of the Government in 1958. And we were advocating that solution openly in the public opinion. And, after that, the Congress had a mediation that didn't succeed because of the gangsterism, subversion of the Castro and the Communist movement – that threatened any people, even in the opposition, that were threatening the pressmen, since the Sierra Maestra, that were threatening to kill anybody that were opposing the solution – the only solution of the Communist Party under the Fidelista movement was having – that is silence in order to get power as they got.

Senator KEATING. Let me ask you a question. You referred to Fidel Castro as, I think you said, the most prominent member of the Communist International movement in the Western Hemisphere but probably or not a card-carrying Communist. Now, were you in law school with Fidel Castro?

Mr. DIAZ BALART. Yes, sir.

Senator KEATING. Can you tell us anything about his activities there of a political character?

Mr. DIAZ BALART. Yes. Right when he started at the university, in 1945, it was very easy for him, and at the same time for the Communists that had and always have had a very powerful branch in the University of Havana – it was very easy for both of them to get to very nice understanding, because Communists know –

Senator DODD. I think if you just answer the question – don't give the reasons why. Senator Keating may want to know them later. But tell what he did and what he said.

Mr. DIAZ BALART. Yes. About what?

Senator KEATING. About his political activities when you were in law school with him.

Mr. DIAZ BALART. Well, he started, as I told you, as a juvenile delinquent, he started killing our fellow students, and united with the Communists, and going in any activity as a front man of the Communists. He had a very well understanding with the Communist movement, because they needed a front man, and Fidel needed them to back him.

Senator KEATING. Was he recognized by the other students as acting in that capacity at the time?

Mr. DIAZ BALART. Oh, yes. But he was always very much careful not to appear. And also the Communist – in order not to appear as Communist.

Senator DODD. How do you know he was a Communist when he was a student?

Mr. DIAZ BALART. I knew that he started together with them, because I knew who were the Communists by name. They were open.

Senator DODD. Were you told this by others?

Mr. DIAZ BALART. No, I knew that by myself.

Senator DODD. You saw him associating with them. Do you know

he was a member? How do you know that?

Mr. DIAZ BALART. No, he was not in that moment a member. He as just in that moment an opportunist leader that wanted to promote himself.

Senator DODD. So your answer is he was associated with people you think were Communists?

Mr. DIAZ BALART. No. In that moment he was associated with people that I know were Communists, because they told to everybody.

Senator DODD. He associated with them. Do you know any more than that?

Mr. DIAZ BALART. And after that, in that procedure, was that when they started to be very useful to each other. I know all the process, because I had to leave the country in 1947 to come to the United States, because I was opposed to Castro.

Senator DODD. We know that. Tell us any more you know.

Mr. DIAZ BALART. About his Communist activities?

Senator DODD. Yes, about Castro when he was a student at the university. That is what Senator Keating asked you.

Mr. DIAZ BALART. Exactly he told me that he was going to go with the Communists because it was the best way for a young leader that was thinking in the future to promote himself to the highest rank.

Senator DODD. Castro told you that?

Mr. DIAZ BALART. Yes.

Senator DODD. All right. That is an answer to the question. What else?

Mr. SOURWINE. Did you know Leonel Soto?

Mr. DIAZ BALART. Yes.

Mr. SOURWINE. Was he a Communist?

Mr. DIAZ BALART. Yes, he was an open leader of the Communist movement.

Mr. SOURWINE. What, if any, were Castro's dealings with him?

Mr. DIAZ BALART. He was also always very well connected to him, and to other Communists.

Mr. SOURWINE. Do you know Alfredo Guevara?

Mr. DIAZ BALART. Yes, sir.

Mr. SOURWINE. Is that the same as "Che" Guevara?

Mr. DIAZ BALART. No, sir.

Mr. SOURWINE. Will you identify Alfredo Guevara?

Mr. DIAZ BALART. Yes, he was a student leader of the Communist branch in Havana University, and of the intellectual branch, and now he is the head of the Cinematographic Institute in Cuba, and the head of the indoctrination program of the Army forces.

Mr. SOURWINE. Is he related to "Che" Guevara?

Mr. DIAZ BALART. I don't think so.

Mr. SOURWINE. Was Castro associated with Alfredo Guevara?

Mr. DIAZ BALART. Yes, sir.

Mr. SOURWINE. Do you know General Pedraza?

Mr. DIAZ BALART. Never I have talked with him.

Mr. SOURWINE. Do you have any knowledge respecting Castro's association with General Pedraza, if any?

Mr DIAZ BALART. General Pedraza?

Mr. SOURWINE. Yes.

Mr. DIAZ BALART. No, I don't know.

Mr. SOURWINE. Did you know Mas Martin?

Mr. DIAZ BALART. Yes.

Mr. SOURWINE. Who was he?

Mr. DIAZ BALART. He was a leader of the Communist youth.

Mr. SOURWINE. Communist youth?

Mr. DIAZ BALART. Yes.

Mr. SOURWINE. Where?

Mr. DIAZ BALART. In Cuba, Havana.

Mr. SOUR WINE. At the Havana University?

Mr. DIAZ BALART. No, in Cuba.

Mr. SOURWINE. While Castro was attending Havana University, was he connected in any way with Mas Martin?

Mr. DIAZ BALART. Yes, in all his activities he was having the backing of the youth movement of the Communist Party that Mas Martin was one of the leaders.

Mr. SOURWINE. Do you know Flavio Bravo?

Mr. DIAZ BALART. Yes.

Mr. SOURWINE. Was he a Communist?

Mr. DIAZ BALART. Yes, he was also a leader of the youth.

Mr. SOURWINE. Was Castro associated with him?

Mr. DIAZ BALART. Yes, sir, also.

Mr. SOURWINE. Do you know a Valdes Vives?

Mr. DIAZ BALART. Valdes Vives? Yes; he was also a well-known Communist leader.

Mr. SOURWINE. Was Castro associated with him?

Mr. DIAZ BALART. Also.

Mr. SOURWINE. Did you know Fabio Grobart?

Mr. DIAZ BALART. Not personally. I knew of his presence in Cuba.

Mr. SOURWINE. Who was he?

Mr. DIAZ BALART. I think from what I heard, he was a, commissar of the Communist movement. Maybe the highest ranking representative of the Third International in Cuba in that moment.

Mr. SOURWINE. Was Grobart a Cuban?

Mr. DIAZ BALART. I don't think so.

Mr. SOURWINE. What was his nationality?

Mr. DIAZ BALART. I think Yugoslav, but I am not sure, because I think that he used to use different names.

Mr. SOURWINE. Do you know where he is now?

Mr. DIAZ BALART. I don't know.

Mr. SOURWINE. Was he ever associated with Castro, or vice versa?

Mr. DIAZ BALART. Well, I think through these other people that you have –

Mr. SOURWINE. Please, not what you think. Do you know?

Mr. DIAZ BALART. No.

Mr. SOURWINE. Did you know one Leonel Gomez?

Mr. DIAZ BALART. Yes, I know who he was.

Mr. SOURWINE. Who was he?

Mr. DIAZ BALART. He was the leader of the secondary institute of Havana.

(At this point, Senator Keating withdrew from the hearing room.)

Mr. SOURWINE. Was be the president of the student body in Havana No. 1 High School?

Mr. DIAZ BALART. That is right.

Mr. SOURWINE. Is he alive now?

Mr. DIAZ BALART. Yes.

Mr. SOURWINE. He is still alive?

Mr. DIAZ BALART. He is still alive.

Mr. SOURWINE. Do you recall that he was shot in 1947 on Ronda Street in Havana?

Mr. DIAZ BALART. Yes, sir.

Mr. SOURWINE. Do you know who shot, him?

Mr. DIAZ BALART. Yes, sir. Fidel Castro.

Mr. SOURWINE. How do you know this?

Mr. DIAZ BALART. Because Fidel Castro told me that. He invited me to participate with him in the killing of that student, and I refused, because I am a Christian, I am against killing, and besides that, there was not any reason to.

Mr. SOURWINE. Why did he want to kill Gomez?

Mr. DIAZ BALART. Because he thought at that moment that Gomez, being a personal friend of President [Grau San] Martin, at that moment the President of Cuba, he was going to be a big obstacle before the ambition of Castro.

Mr. SOURWINE. Was Gomez a Communist?

Mr. DIAZ BALART. No; I do not think so.

Mr. SOURWINE. Was he an anti-Communist?

Mr. DIAZ BALART. I think so.

Mr. SOURWINE. Now, was Castro in your home immediately after the shooting of Gomez?

Mr. DIAZ BALART. Yes, sir.

Mr. SOURWINE. What was he doing there?

Mr. DIAZ BALART. He was trying to hide.

Mr. SOURWINE. He was there by your invitation?

Mr. DIAZ BALART. No; he was there because he was my friend.

Mr. SOURWINE. Did you know Manolo Castro?

Mr. DIAZ BALART. Yes.

Mr. SOURWINE. Was he any relation to Fidel Castro?

Mr. DIAZ BALART. No; no relation.

Mr. SOURWINE. Who was Manolo Castro?

Mr. DIAZ BALART. He was the leader and president of the Federation of University Students of Havana University, a great leader of the student body.

Mr. SOURWINE. Is he alive?

Mr. DIAZ BALART. No; he was killed by Castro.

Mr. SOURWINE. By Castro?

Mr. DIAZ BALART. Yes.

Mr. SOURWINE. Personally?

Mr. DIAZ BALART. I think so.

Mr. SOURWINE. How did he kill him?

Mr. DIAZ BALART. It was in the middle of a street in Havana. This was very much publicized by all the papers in Havana. And Castro before, some weeks before, had told publicly in Havana University that he was going to kill Manolo Castro.

Mr. SOURWINE. You told us that Fidel Castro had told you that he had shot Leonel Gomez. Did he ever tell you anything about killing Manolo Castro?

Mr. DIAZ BALART. No; I was not in Havana then.

Mr. SOURWINE. You did not see the murder?

Mr. DIAZ BALART. No.

Mr. SOURWINE. Was Fidel Castro ever accused of this murder?

Mr. DIAZ BALART. Yes; very much. He had to go before the court.

Mr. SOURWINE. Was he tried for the murder?

Mr. DIAZ BALART. No.

Mr. SOURWINE. You said he had to go before the court. What did you mean?

Mr. DIAZ BALART. In the preliminary procedures of the court – but he did not continue with that. He went, to Bogota at that moment.

Mr. SOURWINE. Fidel Castro went to Bogota?

Mr. DIAZ BALART. Yes.

Mr. SOURWINE. Did the Court absolve him of the killing of Manolo Castro?

Mr. DIAZ BALART. No. I think it was not held – the hearing was not held.

Mr. SOURWINE. Did you know Fernandez Caral?

Mr. DIAZ BALART. Yes; he was a sergeant of the police body of the Havana University.

Mr. SOURWINE. Is he still alive?

Mr. DIAZ BALART. No; he was killed by Fidel Castro.

Mr. SOURWINE. How do you know this?

Mr. Diaz BALART. Because Fidel Castro had told to all my friends after he killed Castro that he was going to have to kill Fernandez Caral, because the sergeant had told that he was going to put Fidel in jail because of the previous killing.

Mr. SOURWINE. Do you have any personal knowledge respecting the killing of Caral?

Mr. DIAZ BALART. No; through my brothers, and through the other friend – I was not in Havana.

Mr. SOURWINE. You have no personal knowledge?

Mr. DIAZ BALART. No personal knowledge.

Mr. SOURWINE. Do you know Carlos Rafael Rodriguez?

Mr. DIAZ BALART. I know who he is.

Mr. SOURWINE. You do not know him personally?

Mr. DIAZ BALART. No.

Mr. SOURWINE. Who is he?

Mr. DIAZ BALART. He is one, of the biggest leaders of the Communist Party in Cuba, the intellectual branch.

Mr. SOURWINE. Does he have, any connection with Fidel Castro?

Mr. DIAZ BALART. Yes; I think that he is a very close adviser of Fidel Castro, and he is the editor of the newspaper Hoy, the official newspaper of the Communist Party in Cuba today. Incidentally, he was just given by the Government a position for the first time in Havana University, an open Communist, a position of professor of economics that was created by him especially.

Mr. SOURWINE. Do you know Raul Castro?

Mr. DIAZ BALART. Yes, sir.

Mr. SOURWINE. He is Fidel Castro's brother?

Mr. DIAZ BALART. Yes, Sir. Mr. SOURWINE. Do you know whether he is a Communist?

Mr. DIAZ BALART. He is a very well trained Communist agent.

Mr. SOURWINE. How do yon know this?

Mr. DIAZ BALART. Because he went to Prague, after he had already become a member of the Communist movement, ideology – he was trained there. When he came back, he was got by the police in the airport with Communist propaganda, and when he was released from the prison, he talked with my brother, Waldo, and he, told to him that he was in prison, but that he was ready not only to be in prison, but to die for the Communist cause.

Mr. SOURWINE. Do you how Raul Castro became a Communist?

Mr. DIAZ BALART. Yes, because Fidel Castro put him in contact with the intellectual machinery of the Communist Party, being Raul a very young man, and they indoctrinated him.

Mr. SOURWINE. Do you remember telling us that Fidel Castro gave his brother Raul copies of Marx's works?

Mr. DIAZ BALART. Yes. That was part of the indoctrination that I just told you.

Mr. SOURWINE. How do you know he did?

Mr. DIAZ BALART. Because I was there, and I knew both of them.

Mr. SOURWINE. Do you know how it came about that Raul Castro met "Che" Guevara?

Mr. DIAZ BALART. I think that was in Mexico, through Raul Castro and through other Communists, Cuban and Mexican.

Mr. SOURWINE. Do you know how this came about? Not what you think – do you know?

Mr. DIAZ BALART. No, I was not in Mexico at that moment.

Mr. SOURWINE. Do you know Vera Lestovna de Zalka?

Mr. DIAZ BALART. Yes.

Mr. SOURWINE. Who is she?

Mr. DIAZ BALART. Not personally.

Mr. SOURWINE. Not personally. Who is she?

Mr. DIAZ BALART. I think she is a, very high ranking member of the Communist machinery in America, in Latin America, through the diplomatic ways.

Mr. SOURWINE. Do you know this to be true?

Mr. DIAZ BALART. I cannot assure, you; I think. I have the impression. To me it is sure, but not to tell officially to the committee.

Mr. SOURWINE. Does she have diplomatic connections?

Mr. DIAZ BALART. Pardon Me?

Mr. SOURWINE. Does she have diplomatic connections?

Mr. DIAZ BALART. Yes; I think she is the wife of a Hungarian Ambassador in South America.

Mr. SOURWINE. Do you know what country?

Mr. DIAZ BALART. I think this is in Argentina. All that story has been published in the very well-known magazine, Vanguardia, by one of the ranking Communist writers of South America, Mr. Rudolfo Alvenas.

Mr. SOURWINE. Do you know of any connection between Fidel Castro and this woman?

Mr. DIAZ BALART. Not. exactly. I know the connection of Fidel Castro throughout Latin America. Maybe, I think that Fidel Castro now is more important than any other agent in Latin America.

Mr. SOURWINE. Do you recall giving us the names of two Russians whom you said arrived in Cuba in May 1959, to inaugurate a new type of labor movement in South America?

Mr. DIAZ BALART. Yes, I recall that. That was almost a year ago.

Mr. SOURWINE. Who were those two Russians?

Mr. DIAZ BALART. I think the name Timofei, and another name I do not recall, because I do not have a very good memory of Russian names.

Mr. SOURWINE. One, name you gave us is Eremev Timofei?

Mr. DIAZ BALART. That is right.

Mr. SOURWINE, And the other name you gave us Ivan Arapov?,

Mr. DIAZ BALART. I think so; yes

Mr. SOURWINE. Did you or didn't you?

Mr. DIAZ BALART. Pardon me?

Mr. SOURWINE. Did you give us those names?

Mr. DIAZ BALART. Yes.

Mr. SOURWINE. How did you know of the arrival of those two Russian in Cuba ?

Mr. DIAZ BALART. I was informed by my underground movement that they were in a specific hotel, for one of the people that was serving them was a member of my movement.

Mr. SOURWINE. Are you able to tell us how Fidel Castro was able to get support and money for his revolution?

Mr. DIAZ BALART. I think there was something like a circle, working out above all through very nice propaganda. Of course, some of the situation of the regime in that moment was, naturally, maybe helping him. And through a very well – by a very well integrate propaganda – for example, some articles by Herbert Matthews, of the New York Times, that were helping him very much, was in the Sierra Maestra, at the beginning of Castro, and he published in the New York Times that he had seen personally hundreds and hundreds of very well trained soldiers, was a high morale, anti-Communist, and so forth.

And now the Castro people had published, after they got power, and there is in the Cuban magazines, that in that moment they just had about 12 or 13 men. And propaganda like this – you can see that they were given the impression that they had already a very strong movement, a very high moral movement, and so forth.

And I think that the Communists got the idea that there was an opportunity to help that movement.

Mr. SOURWINE. Did the 26th of July Movement have support from the United States before Castro's regime came to power?

Mr. DIAZ BALART. A lot of support.

Mr. SOURWINE. Where was that support centered, if you know?

Mr. DIAZ BALART. Pardon me, sir?

Mr. SOURWINE. Where was that support centered, if you know?

Mr. DIAZ BALART. Well, I think that it was centered in New York City, in Miami, and even they got some help from the naval base in Guantanamo.

Mr. SOURWINE. Do you know where, the headquarters of the 26th of July Movement in New York City is?

Mr. DIAZ BALART. Right now it is in the Belvedere Hotel.

Mr. SOURWINE. The Belvedere Hotel?

Mr. DIAZ BALART. The Belvedere; yes, sir.

Mr. SOURWINE. That is 319 West 49th Street, New York City?

Mr. DIAZ BALART. Yes, I think so. Yes. Sir.

Air. SOURWINE. Can you name any of the persons in this country who are presently working for Castro, outside of the Cuban Embassy?

Mr. DIAZ BALART. Besides the people of the Embassy?

Mr. SOURWINE. Outside.

Mr. DIAZ BALART. Outside, yes.

Although they are not any more registered in the Justice Department, they represent the Cuban Government – they have had headquarters, as I told, in Hotel Belvedere.

There is a Secretary General called Mr. Jose Sanchez. They have a link through a man called Jose Vazquez. And they give money through the consulate and through the Cubana Airlines. They have, according to their own statement published in the newspaper – they have what they call commando actions in New York City and Miami, that they use in New York City and Miami, in order to threaten every Cuban that is against Castro, that is not a Communist, and is not pro-Castro.

Mr. SOURWINE. Do you have any information respecting the use of violence by the 26th of July organization to break up a celebration in Central Park in honor of Jose Marti in January of this year?

Mr. DIAZ BALART. Yes, Sir.

Mr. SOURWINE. What do you know about that?

Mr. DIAZ BALART. Pardon me?

Mr. SOURWINE. What do you know about the use of violence on that occasion?

Mr. DIAZ BALART. Well, the White Rose organization asked for a permit to the Police Department of New York City in order to put a wreath of flowers before the Marti monument in Central Park South, and when we were arriving there having the wreath, we were attacked and the police of New York were attacked by them, by a bunch of gangsters headed by a man named Hector Duarte, who is a cop killer, that had arrived before with a diplomat passport. And the police of New York, although they questioned him, was not able, to act because of the diplomatic passport. And they started attacking also with irons and stones and so forth. And after that they published in the Revolution newspaper the picture of the act and how these people received orders from the commando action in order to attack violently us. And in fact there was the intention to kill Colonel Merob Sosa and myself.

Mr. SOURWINE. Does the 26th of July Movement conduct fund-raising activities in the United States, to your knowledge?

Mr. DIAZ BALART. Yes. I have a card of one of the acts that they had in 691 Columbus Avenue, between 93d and 94th Street in New York, Saturday, 23d of April, for instance, where they are electing a Queen of the Land Reform in New York – 50 cents every one of these cards.

Mr. SOURWINE. Do you have any knowledge respecting a meeting of the 26th of July Movement at 914 Prospect Avenue in the Bronx, on April 22, 1960?

Mr. DIAZ BALART. Yes, Sir. There was there talking the Consul Rogelio Guillot and Mr. Jose Vazquez.

Mr. SOURWINE. Do you have any knowledge regarding a meeting held in Union Square, New York City, May 1, 1960?

Mr. DIAZ BALART. Yes. At that meeting a special agent of the Communist movement in the labor organization of Cuba, Mr.

Gustavo Mas, arrived there to address in that meeting in Union Square on the question of Negro unrest in the United States, and the question of the independence of Puerto Rico, and other international and national questions of the United States of America, in order to start a movement that they have been organizing very well to provoke troubles within the United States.

Mr. SOURWINE. Was this meeting in Union Square held under the auspices of the 26tb of July Movement?

Mr. DIAZ BALART. I am not sure what auspices, because I was already here in Washington. I think that was the 26th of July Movement, or some American organization. I am not sure about that. I know that Gustavo Mas was there and talked about these things.

Mr. SOURWINE. Who is Gustavo Mas?

Mr. DIAZ BALART. He is a high-ranking labor leader of the Communist movement in Cuba.

Mr. SOURWINE. Do you know what Fidel Castro's aim is with regard to the United States?

Mr. DIAZ BALART. Yes. I think – I mean I know that the Communists, as any man that studies a little bit of the procedure of the Communists, they know by elementary knowledge of the geopolitics that it is not possible to have a common state here in the Western Hemisphere. So it has been published very much, they have the theory of what they call terra arras sol, that is to say, I think, the theory of the complete destruction of the land, which is the theory of Mao Tse-tung the Communist leader, which, is one of the best theoretical minds of the Communist movement, and that is what they are trying to do in Cuba, to destroy absolutely the land and to provoke from Cuba a struggle within the United States, taking advantage of some situations in the United States – taking advantage of some situation between the United States and other countries of Latin America, and to promote a revolution, or if not a revolution at least a struggle, a provocation, a big fighting, within the United States and in other countries of Latin America.

Mr. SOURWINE. Do I understand correctly that through your organization, the White Rose, you have an information flow from Cuba to you? You get information from Cuba?

Mr. DIAZ BALART. Yes; quite often.

Mr. SOURWINE. Does this information give you any knowledge respecting the aims of the Castro regime as against other countries in Latin America?

Mr. DIAZ BALART. Yes. They have got already a very good base in Cuba, which they are using as a center for the provocation in all Latin America, and in the United States, and between the United States and Latin America.

Mr. SOURWINE. A provocation of what?

Mr. DIAZ BALART. Struggles confusion, troubles. For instance, there is a situation in the Negro problem in some of the United States, that only those States maybe understand. Now, that has been having a peculiar situation, and what would happen if – what would happen if some provocateurs, Communist provocateurs, try to form mobs, besides the natural feeling of those that I do not judge, because I am not a citizen of this country.

Besides that is the very well-trained Communist agitator, go there and start mobs, and that mob start, exercise violence, like they have done in other countries, when it would be necessary to have one killing – that killing starts more violence and more bad feelings. And that is the way that they work all throughout the world.

As an example – we have examples throughout the world now.

Mr. SOURWINE. I have no further questions.

Senator DODD. Very well. You may be excused. Thank you very much.

Mr. DIAZ BALART. Thank you very much.